"With clear and concise writing, the author demystifies the complex web of culture and religion that characterizes the American Church and illuminates why the variety of ethnic and generational cultures can create a dissonant and polarized ecclesiastic reality. On that foundation, she offers practical and insightful ways for responding to the dissonance and creating a multicultural harmony and communion."

—William A. Nordenbrock, CPPS, author of *Beyond Accompaniment: Guiding a Fractured Community to Wholeness*

"The two major themes of *Catholic Cultures* match exactly the two most trenchant concerns in parishes—shifting ethnic configurations and generational changes among parishioners. Through the lens of culture, Patricia Wittberg briefly traces the history of ethnic groups in the US and explains the current situation. Her cogent description of how generational relationships affect parish life is accompanied by suggestions of 'welcoming practices' designed to incorporate Catholic Millennials. The author offers parish leaders hope and encouragement as they seek to respond to evolving parish contexts."

—Katarina Schuth, OSF, author of *Seminary Formation: Recent History—Current Circumstances—New Directions*

"Sister Patricia Wittberg's new book is essential reading for those who wish to better serve the People of God, and for all those who wish to continue growing as well informed Catholics. Wittberg brings both a rich history of what each culture has brought to Catholicism in times past as well as a modern day awareness of how efforts can be made to see the Church through many different cultural lenses today. Her insightful research illustrates how we can all evolve from a mere tolerance of our differences to becoming enriched by the beauty that each culture brings to our common heritage of faith. I highly recommend this enlightening work to Catholics of all generations, ethnicities, and cultural backgrounds."

—Stephen Fichter, CARA Research Associate and co-author of *Same Call Different Men: The Evolution of the Priesthood since Vatican II*

D1616486

"Finally we have a book a book about parish ministry that doesn't pretend that our parishes have not been radically refigured by immigration, ethnic and racial diversity, and sweeping generational disaffiliation. For too long, parish renewal literature has assumed that cultural and generational differences were only marginal issues in our parishes. Sr. Patricia Wittberg, sociologist and pastoral thinker, rightly identifies these as the central issues of our time. One of the principal strengths of the book is her refusal to underestimate the complexity and challenges of ministry across cultures and generational divides, making use of the sociology of culture to navigate these difficult waters. Another strength is her willingness to look at the ethnic and cultural differences *within* generational groups."

— Brett C. Hoover
Assistant Professor of Theological Studies
Loyola Marymount University, Los Angeles

Catholic Cultures

How Parishes Can Respond
to the Changing Face of Catholicism

Patricia Wittberg, SC

LITURGICAL PRESS
Collegeville, Minnesota

www.litpress.org

1	2	3	4	5	6	7	8	9

Library of Congress Cataloging-in-Publication Data

Wittberg, Patricia, 1947-
  Catholic cultures : how parishes can respond to the changing face of Catholicism / Patricia Wittberg.
    pages   cm
    ISBN 978-0-8146-4858-2 — ISBN 978-0-8146-4883-4 (ebook)
    1. Church work with minorities—Catholic Church.   2. Multiculturalism—Religious aspects—Catholic Church.   3. Catholic Church—United States—Membership.   I. Title.

BX2347.8.I46W57   2015
282'.7308—dc23   2015006943

Contents

Introduction

"At this sound, they gathered in a large crowd, but they were confused because each one heard them speaking in his own language."

—Acts 2:6

The birth of the church at Pentecost as recounted in Acts reveals a unique difference between Christianity and many other religious traditions. From its very beginning, the Gospel message was announced, not exclusively in the Aramaic language that Jesus himself spoke, nor in Hebrew, nor even in Greek or Latin, but in the native language of each hearer. The Koran, the Talmud and Torah, and the Upanishads are studied and memorized by their respective adherents in the original (and increasingly archaic) languages in which they were first written. Their sacred rituals, too, are often performed with languages, gestures, and symbols that are no longer used or meaningful in everyday life. In contrast, the Good News of Jesus has had its primary impact *when translated into each receiving culture*.

This is not to say that Christianity has been exempt from canonizing an extinct but sacred language, as any Catholic old enough to remember the Latin Mass can attest. Even today, there are varieties of Eastern Orthodox Christianity whose liturgical language has remained unchanged for centuries, if not millennia. Having a sacred language can be beneficial: it sets the time of worship apart from daily, "profane" life and helps the worshipper enter into a spirit of prayer. But in the process, what was fresh and challenging and prophetic to the original followers may become a fossilized set of half-understood rituals. Worse still, if a religious tradition becomes too identified with one particular language, or one particular way to worship, or one particular constellation of saints, festivals, and symbols, its followers may be less willing and less able to spread it to other cultures—or even to retain the next generation of their own culture as it changes around them.

The goal of this book is to explore what it would mean for each parish to take the Pentecost story in Acts seriously. How can Catholics proclaim the Good News in the native language(s) of newcomers whose backgrounds may be quite different from their own? It may seem difficult—or even impossible—to do so, and dangerous to try. All cultures are human creations, and therefore all cultures are imperfect. Enfleshing the Good News in any human culture will necessarily incorporate some of that culture's imperfections, and it is those outside the culture who will be the most aware of these deficiencies (while simultaneously, of course, being blind to the ways in which their *own* interpretation of the Gospel truths falls short). But Catholics are called—as the apostles were called—to speak the Good News, however imperfectly, in every time and culture. It takes faith and trust in the guidance of the Pentecostal Spirit to do this and not to retreat into our own familiar ways of "being Catholic."

A Brief Introduction to "Culture"

What is "culture" anyway? In popular speech, the word usually refers to some artistic activity: we attend "cultural events" such as a symphony, a play, or an exhibit of paintings at a gallery or museum. Persons living in areas with a recent immigrant population may be exposed to its food, dances, or music at "multicultural" festivals. But "culture" includes deeper and wider dimensions as well.

Very little of what makes us human is inborn in us. From our very first days of life, we are absorbing a culture. Even in the womb, we hear the rhythms and inflections of the languages our mothers are speaking, and tests show that newborns can distinguish the language they heard *in utero* from an unfamiliar one. In early childhood we absorb not only our spoken language but an entire vocabulary of behaviors, values, beliefs, and assumptions that make us think like, act like, and *be* Americans (or Nigerians, Chinese, Brazilians, Italians, etc.). By the time we are adults, our culture has become like the air we breathe—we don't even notice that it is there unless some person (or some event, like moving to another country) makes us conscious of it. The subtle and subconscious aspects of culture are especially hard to notice—and especially hard to change.

Culture has many different dimensions, each of which spans the range from the obvious and known to the hidden and subconscious:

- *The Material Dimension of Culture* includes concrete places and artifacts that can be touched, tasted, or seen. This includes objects such as clocks, automobiles, clothing, and the numerous electronic gadgets that clutter our lives. It also includes the spatial arrangements of our homes, workplaces, and neighborhoods. Some aspects of material culture give obvious messages, but many have a hidden symbolic dimension as well. The kind of car you drive, whether you occupy the corner office or a small cubicle, whether (and where) you sport a tattoo—all give out particular messages about you. The smallest detail signals to others your membership in a given in-group, or out-group.

- *The Behavioral Dimension of Culture* includes ways people act. This includes, first of all, norms and rules about the way one is expected to dress, talk, walk, greet others, make eye contact, touch another person (or not!), and so forth. It also includes jokes, gossip, slang, and jargon (and when to engage in them). Finally, behavioral culture includes rituals, both formal ones that mark specific events such as birthdays, holidays, or retirement, and informal ones such as shaking hands upon meeting someone or greeting a colleague in the hallway at work. The behavioral rules may be explicitly expressed or left unsaid, and sometimes the unspoken rules contradict the spoken ones.

- *The Value Dimension of Culture* includes shared definitions of what is right or wrong, beautiful or ugly, desirable or undesirable. This includes preferred personality characteristics (Should women, or men, be shy and retiring? Aggressive? Ambitious? Ruthless? Considerate?) and goals (Should we strive for financial success? Intra-group harmony? Mystical experiences?). It also includes the emotional "tone" attached to situations, objects, words, concepts. In some cultures it is a compliment to call something "new" or "government-run," while in other cultures these attributes are viewed with great suspicion. Being a "liberal" or a "feminist" may be avant-garde at one time or in one place but considered out-of-date elsewhere (or elsewhen).

- Finally, *the Cognitive Dimension of Culture* includes shared definitions of reality. These assumptions are usually so subconscious that we are rarely aware of them, but they form the basis for even the most mundane of our decisions:

  - How do we determine what is true? By pragmatic test? By the wisdom of the elders? By group consensus?

  - What is the nature of time? Is it cyclic or linear? Is linear time progressing toward a better future or regressing toward a worse one? Which is the most relevant aspect of time to consider when making decisions: the past? the present? the future?

- What about human nature? Are humans basically good, neutral, or bad? Is human nature fixed or is it able to be improved? Are outsiders benign or threatening, trustworthy or untrustworthy?
- What or who is to blame when something goes wrong? Why do bad things happen to good people?
- What beliefs "go together"? Can I oppose gun control and still be a feminist? Enjoy watching "Duck Dynasty" and still eat arugula salads? Believe in both global warming and stricter immigration enforcement?
- Finally, cognitive culture includes the shared meanings of words. What specific activities or situations are included in the term "justice"? Or "pro-life"? Or "terrorism"?

From birth, we absorb all of these dimensions of our culture from our surrounding society: from our families, our neighborhoods, our friends, the mass media, school, etc. Cultures therefore differ—to a greater or lesser extent—from ethnic group to ethnic group, from one socioeconomic class to another, and across generations. The more distant another culture is from ours, especially in its behavioral, value, and cognitive dimensions, the more difficult it will be for us to understand each other. This has many implications for Catholics today. To the extent that our parishes are increasingly composed of members from different ethnic groups, ages, or social classes, it may become more difficult for parish staff to translate the Good News of Jesus into languages/values/concepts that speak to each of the parish's different cultures. In addition, Catholic parents today are only too aware of the gap between their own childhood experiences and those of their children, and frequently find that "being Catholic" doesn't seem to be as important to their sons and daughters as it is to them—if, indeed, their offspring are interested in remaining in the church at all.

Ethnic Cultures in the Church

It is vital that church ministers and church members find ways to speak the Good News to these different cultures. In welcoming different racial and ethnic groups, we are emulating the example of the apostles in the Pentecost story of Acts. Additionally, current demographic changes in the American church mandate that we do so, or our parishes will lose the greater part of their membership and vitality. A brief glance at Figure 1 shows why:

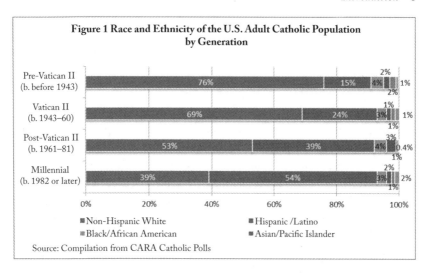

Figure 1 Race and Ethnicity of the U.S. Adult Catholic Population by Generation

Source: Compilation from CARA Catholic Polls

We can see that, while three-fourths of the oldest American Catholics are non-Hispanic whites, only 39 percent of the youngest Catholic adults belong to this ethnic group. In contrast, over half of the youngest adult age cohort is Hispanic—something that is true of only 15 percent of the oldest age cohort.

Ethnic change, of course, is not new to the American Catholic Church. In the early- to mid-nineteenth century, the extremely small population of English-descended Catholics in the United States (and its largely French clergy who had fled from anticlerical Revolutionary France) was overwhelmed by an influx of Irish immigrants—people with a very different ethnic culture and from a much lower social class. In parts of the Midwest, large populations of German Catholic immigrants lived in an uneasy truce with their Irish neighbors. Bishops and clergy, both in this country and in Europe, fretted that, if these new immigrants' needs for catechesis, education, health care, and social services were not met, they would desert Catholicism for Protestant churches. This fear was the impetus for the founding of separate parishes for each ethnic group, as well as separate Catholic systems of schools, hospitals, and social agencies. It also motivated the political jockeying of Irish and German immigrant clergy for power within the nineteenth-century American hierarchy. In later years, the church absorbed incoming Italians, French Canadians, Poles, Slovenes, Slovaks, and a host of other groups by following the same pattern: establishing parishes and grade schools for each ethnicity that were staffed by communities of religious sisters drawn from the old country.

By the time Hispanic migrants from Mexico, Puerto Rico, Cuba, and other parts of Latin America began to arrive in the mid-twentieth century, however, the church had reconsidered this policy. The 1950s and 1960s Civil Rights Movement had sensitized Catholics to the problems involved in creating "separate but equal" parishes for different ethnic groups. Catholics, both clergy and lay, began to feel that integrating new arrivals into existing parishes was the better option. Critics later charged, however, that this had relegated Hispanics to second-class status: attending Masses in the church basement while Anglos worshipped in the main church, and being excluded from parish decision making. Alternatively, if the Hispanics came to outnumber the Anglos in a parish, Spanish-language liturgies began to be scheduled in the main worship space and at the "best" times, leaving the older, non-Hispanic members feeling increasingly disenfranchised. Things became even more interesting if, in addition to Hispanic and Anglo parishioners, the parish also included Vietnamese, Filipinos, Nigerians, or other groups.

Generational Cultures in the Church

While it is important to consider the challenges that various ethnic cultures pose for Catholic parishes, it is also important to consider *generational cultures*. Many people may not be used to considering members of different generations as separate cultural groups, but the age cohorts in our parishes display behavioral, value, and cognitive differences from each other that may be as pastorally challenging as ethnic differences are. Just as specific experiences drawn from a particular ethnic culture influence the children who grow up in that culture—shaping the language(s) they speak, the food they like, and the value they place on educational achievement, machismo, or close family ties—so, too, the particular time period in which a person is born and passes his/her childhood also leaves an indelible mark. For example, the material artifacts available to a child—radio, TV, cell phones, iPads—will affect how that child relates to others, how quickly he/she becomes aware of the latest fads, and even, according to the latest research, how he/she thinks and learns. The spatial arrangements of material culture—whether, for example, one grows up in an older neighborhood with sidewalks and an interconnected grid of streets or in a gated subdivision of cul-de-sacs separated from other areas by a busy highway— will affect how widely children can explore on their own, as compared to having their parents drive them everywhere. National and international events also leave their mark: growing up in times of scarcity such as the Great Depression of the 1930s or the Great

Recession that followed 2008 had a different impact on children than passing one's childhood in relatively prosperous times such as the 1950s or 1990s.

There are more subtle effects, too. While people typically cannot remember anything that happened in the larger world before they were five or six years old, these events can still influence their cultural outlook *because they influenced their parents and teachers.* Parents who had learned in their own youth that dollars were scarce, or that the United States was always on the good side of any war it engaged in, or that priests and religious were "better" than laypeople in turn gave this message to their children—even if economic, political, or church events had rendered these beliefs less applicable in the child's world.

According to sociologist Karl Mannheim, children and young adolescents typically accept the culture—the material artifacts, the rules and behaviors, the values, and, especially, the basic grounding beliefs and assumptions—that their parents had taught them through their words and unconscious example. The children might not have understood *why* Communists were bad, or *why* they had to be extra polite to priests and nuns, or *why* they spent all their time in CCD making collages and drawing rainbows; that was just the way things were.

Around the age of twenty, however, young adults reach a critical stage of cognitive maturity, when they can evaluate for themselves the strengths and weaknesses of the culture they had acquired in childhood:

- How could America claim to be such a good country when it denied civil rights to African Americans or waged war in Vietnam?

- What was the sense in building up a savings account instead of going into debt, when the inflation of the 1970s was reducing the value of both savings and IOUs?

- Was scientific "progress" really a good thing—as our water and air filled with toxic chemicals, our nuclear power plants melted down, and our space shuttles spectacularly exploded?

Sometimes (but not always) these growing doubts were crystallized by specific events: Pearl Harbor, the Kennedy assassination, the Second Vatican Council, the Challenger explosion, 9/11. At other times, there was no crystallizing event to mark the transition to a new generational mindset, and the generations tended to shift gradually from one to another. Persons born on the "cusp" between generations often do not exactly identify with either one.

According to Mannheim, for the rest of our lives the way we see the world is colored by the experiences and assumptions we unconsciously absorbed as children, and by how we reacted to these experiences as we entered our twenties:

> All later experiences thus tend to receive their meaning from this original set, whether they appear as its verification and fulfillment or its negation and antithesis . . . Any two generations following one another always fight different opponents, both within and without. While the older people may still be fighting one battle, in such a fashion that all their feelings and efforts and even their concepts and categories of thought are determined by that adversary, for the younger people, this adversary may be simply non-existent: their primary orientation is an entirely different one.[1]

The mixture of the unconscious assumptions and values we absorbed in childhood, and our critical reaction to some—*but not all*—of these assumptions when we reach adulthood, gives each generation a particular and unique cultural outlook. Furthermore, generational cultures overlap with ethnic cultures, regional cultures, class-based cultures, and lifestyle cultures. White Americans, African Americans, and Hispanic Americans—or working-class, middle-class, and upper-class Americans—will each display unique generational differences between their old and young members. We cannot assume that young White Americans will experience the same crystallizing events or have the same generational cultures as Hispanics or African Americans their same age.

For Catholicism today, generational cultures may be the most important of all. A given parish may be—and often has been in the past—composed of only one ethnic/racial group or only one social class, but *no parish can be alive and vibrant for very long if it draws its members from only one generation.* As Figure 2 makes clear, Catholics today are increasingly drawn from the Millennial (born after 1982) and the post-Vatican II (born between 1961 and 1981) generations. By definition, they do not remember the Second Vatican Council, much less the pre-Vatican II church that had formed their elders. In addition, a much larger percentage of these young adult Catholics are Hispanic, Asian, or African American. What is the "language" the church needs to use—the catechesis, the prayer forms, the images, the opportunities for spiritual growth—to speak the Good News to them?

Figure 2
The Generational Composition of American Catholicism:
1987 and 2011

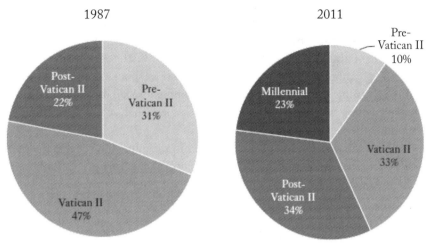

1987   2011

Source: D'Antonio, Dillon, and Gautier, 2013, p. 30.

The Dangers of Cultural Translation

But is this kind of translation really desirable? Jesuit anthropologist William Biernatzki studied how Buddhism, Islam, and Christianity spread from their cultures of origin to the completely different societies of China, Indonesia, and Korea. He noted that translating the worldview and the concepts of a religion into a different cultural context involves difficulties that neither the receiving culture nor the missionary transmitters may be willing or able to surmount. China, for example, never completely adopted Buddhism because the "root paradigms" of Chinese cognitive culture and values—their basic assumptions about the primary importance of filial piety, individual duty, and personal respect (saving "face")—conflicted with Buddhist teachings on monastic celibacy, losing oneself in Nirvana, and begging as a valued ascetical practice. The deeper dimensions of a culture—its values and its basic cognitive assumptions— may be so deeply embedded in the subconscious levels of the hearers' minds as to render the new religious message literally "unthinkable" to them. Even when a foreign culture does adopt the new religion, as Indonesia did Islam, its underlying cognitive culture and values may subtly change the religion's basic "flavor" in a way that the original followers would not approve. "Although Islam 'conquered' Indonesia, it had to surrender much of its Middle Eastern rigor to do so," because Indonesians looked with distaste on anyone who exhibited too much zeal or enthusiasm, even for the sake of religion.[2] *Can* any religion be accurately translated across cultures without losing its original meaning?

Beyond these cognitive cultural differences in root paradigms, specific symbols may also come to have different connotations when imparted to a different culture. Biernatzki notes that Korean Catholics considered the crucifix a symbol of "ugly suffering" and found it "shocking and repulsive." Similarly, calling God "Father" will have a different meaning in a matrilineal society where it is the maternal uncle, not the father, who lives with and supports the family.

With the inevitability of such changes in meaning and tone, many parishioners and parish staff may hesitate to accept the "foreign" Catholicism of another ethnic or generational culture as equal to their own, familiar one. They will be quick to see the imperfections in the new arrivals' interpretation of Catholic teachings and in their way of living Catholicism. *But they will be less aware that their own culture's version of Catholicism is also imperfect.* It is a basic premise of this book that we all can come to a deeper appreciation of the breadth and length, the height and depth, of the Good News by attempting truly to understand the way other cultures besides our own articulate it in their languages, behaviors, values, and cognitive assumptions.

The book's first part will discuss the various ethnic cultures that comprise the American Catholic Church today. After a brief historical overview of these cultures in chapter 1, chapter 2 will describe and compare some of their culturally-specific articulations of the Good News as they have been manifested in American Catholicism both today and in the past. Chapter 3 will outline some of the challenges that these varied versions of Catholicism pose in a multicultural parish, and will advance some practical suggestions for how they might be met.

The second part of the book will follow the same pattern in discussing generational cultures: chapter 4 will describe the various generational cultures in the United States today. Chapter 5 will explore how each generation experiences Catholicism today and will outline some challenges involved in attracting the younger generation to our parishes and making them welcome when they come. Chapter 6 will give practical suggestions on how these challenges might be overcome.

The birth of the church began with the Pentecost experience described in Acts, but it did not end there. The birth of the church is still ongoing. The Gospel message must be born anew in each ethnic and generational culture, and the Holy Spirit has called us—as the apostles were called—to be its midwives.

I

Ethnic Groups in the Catholic Church—Past and Present

"The great God . . . loves the resident alien, giving them food and clothing. So you too should love the resident alien, for that is what you were in the land of Egypt."

—Deuteronomy 10:18-19

The Catholic Church in the United States has always been a church of immigrants. There were only thirty thousand Catholics in the entire country at the end of the colonial period. This small population was engulfed by waves of Irish immigrants in the early nineteenth century, followed by German Catholics in mid-century, and Italian, Polish, French Canadian, and various other nationalities by the turn of the twentieth century. Over four million Irish migrated to the United States during the nineteenth century, and close to two million Germans—although not all of either group were Catholic. By 1900, close to 100,000 Italians were entering the United States every year, primarily from Southern Italy and Sicily. Each wave of newcomers differed in their social class, in their religious knowledge and practice, and in their educational levels. Over half of the Italian immigrants could not read or write their native language, while the majority of the German and Polish immigrants could. The Irish immigrants who had arrived during the famines of the 1830s and 1840s were largely destitute, poorly catechized in the faith, and afflicted with social and familial dysfunctions. Later arrivals from Ireland, while still poor, were better educated and more fervently Catholic, having been influenced by the "Devotional Revolution" that was sweeping Irish Catholicism at the time.[1]

Each group of newcomers tended to settle in different parts of the country, depending on where economic opportunities presented themselves and on where previous migrants from their homeland had settled. Thus, while Irish Catholics were the largest nineteenth-century group overall, there was an equal or greater localized presence of German Catholics in the "German Triangle" stretching between Milwaukee, St. Louis, and Cincinnati. Three-fourths of all the Catholic parishes with German-speaking priests were located within this German Triangle, with the largest proportion in Milwaukee: 40 percent of all Milwaukee parishes were German-speaking. Similarly, while only a tenth as many French Canadian as German Catholic immigrants migrated to the United States, 72 percent of them settled in New England. Poles and other Eastern Europeans arrived between 1880 and 1920 and settled in the burgeoning industrial cities along the Great Lakes. By the middle of the twentieth century, 18 percent of US adult Catholics identified their ancestry as Italian, followed by 16 percent Irish, 13 percent German, 9 percent Polish, 7 percent Mexican, and smaller percentages of other nationalities.[2]

What to do with all of these new arrivals? Initially, the American bishops, who were now predominantly Irish and Irish-American themselves, were wary of constructing separate parishes for them:

> Bishops viewed national parishes as temporary solutions until assimilation permitted a single administrative system and a single Catholic culture, preferably one consonant with that of the Church's Irish majority.[3]

But the immigrants demanded their own parishes, often constructing the church building themselves, and then petitioning the local bishop to provide them with a priest from their nationality group. There were 1,600 explicitly national parishes in the United States by 1912: 346 of which were German, 336 Polish, and 214 Italian.[4] By 1916, almost half of all US Catholics attended a parish where some other language was used—either together with English (28 percent) or as the sole parish language (21 percent).[5] French Canadian parishes grew from fewer than 20 in the 1870s to 178 in 1945. Polish parishes swelled from fewer than 15 in 1870 to over 800 in 1930.[6] "Whereas between 1850 and 1880, only 9% of the new parishes established in the Northeast were national parishes, between 1880 and 1930, 30% were national."[7]

Table 1.1
Parishes Offering Services in Various Foreign Languages, 1916

Language	Number of Parishes	% of Total Number of Parishes	Number of Adherents	% of Total Number of Adherents
French	699	4.6%	1,026,966	6.6%
German	1,890	12.5%	1,672,960	10.7%
Italian	476	3.1%	1,515,818	9.7%
Polish	735	4.8%	1,425,193	9.1%
Spanish	841	5.5%	552,244	3.5%
Bohemian (Czech)	178	1.2%	133,911	0.8%
Lithuanian	96	0.6%	150,227	1.0%
Slavic	113	0.7%	118,264	0.8%
Slovak	109	0.7%	125,687	0.8%
More than one foreign language	839	5.5%	929,719	5.9%
Total # of Ethnic Parishes/Adherents	5,976	39.2%	7,650,989	48.3%
Total # of Catholic Parishes/Adherents	15,163		15,667,700	

Calculated from Roger Finke and Rodney Stark, *The Churching of America, 1776–1990* (New Brunswick, NJ: Rutgers University Press, 1992), 127–129.

Ethnic parishes were valued by their parishioners for several reasons. For one thing, they enabled the immigrants to replicate the village life they had left in their homelands. The German parishes often did this literally, as a large proportion of German immigrants settled in rural areas. Parts of the Midwest are still dotted with small towns clustered around the local Catholic church. Several of these towns are actually named after the church's patron saint: St. Joseph, Indiana, and St. Henry, Ohio, for example. The older inhabitants in some of these areas can still speak the Swabian or Bavarian German dialects of their great-grandparents. In contrast, few of the Irish, French Canadian, or Polish immigrants settled in rural areas, but they were able to replicate their former village life in the city through their parish. "The Catholic parish functioned as a rural village in an urban setting, molding and serving a cohesive social and religious community."[8]

A second function of ethnic parishes, and especially of ethnic parish *schools*, was to pass on the language and culture of the old country to the next generation. For the French Canadian, German, and Polish immigrants, their native languages were inextricably tied with their faith, and they feared losing both in a more secular, Protestant, and English-speaking America. As a result, they constructed their own schools: in 1910 there were 133 French-language schools serving the Canadian immigrants in New England—40 percent of all the Catholic schools in the area.[9] By 1927, there were over 500 Polish Catholic schools, and 73 percent of all Polish-American children were at least partially educated in them.[10] Two-thirds of all German-speaking parishes had constructed schools by 1884, as compared to only one-fourth of the Irish parishes.[11] The pupils in these ethnic Catholic schools learned the history and traditions of their parents' homelands, and at least half of the classes were conducted in languages other than English.[12]

Establishing ethnic parishes also served the interests of the largely Irish-American hierarchy:

> However ingenious the non-English-speaking Catholics proved to be in transforming the national parish into a positive institution of cultural preservation, at the time of its establishment in New York it was intended to separate the pastoral care of the English-speaking Irish and German majority from other Catholics. The practical effect . . . was to keep archdiocesan financial resources at the service of the English-speaking parishes—overwhelmingly Irish. Henceforth, a national parish was virtually orphaned by the archdiocese, left to the financial resources of the religious order [that was staffing it] or the immigrant community, and relegated to a secondary role in archdiocesan attention.[13]

At times, the development of ethnically-homogeneous parishes, schools, and other institutions could be used as a power resource in an immigrant group's interactions with civil and ecclesial authorities. At other times, however, the immigrants keenly felt—and resented—their isolation from the mainstream of the church.

Conflicts

Combining so many different ethnic versions of Catholicism in one church, therefore, was anything but smooth. Conflicts routinely erupted, both within parishes, between different ethnic parishes, and with priests and bishops. On the intra-parish level, a single German, Italian, or Slavic congregation might contain multiple subcultures, each with different linguistic dialects and different devotional customs. Among German Catholic immigrants, for example, 21 percent came from Bavaria, 42 percent from newly-annexed Prussian regions of Westphalia and the Rhineland, and 10 percent from northern German states. One observer noted that "the Saxon does not like the Swabian, nor the Prussian the Bavarian, and the Westphalian would . . . devour the poor Badenser alive, and so conversely."[14] Another historian wrote that German parishioners frequently quarreled with one another over which hymns to sing and where to build their churches. One dispute over hymns became so heated that one side burned down the church building![15] Other ethnic groups, too, were not exempt from intra-parish quarrels. The first Slovak Catholic immigrants came to the United States from Hungary, where they had been an oppressed minority group. After spending their hard-earned money and time building their own parishes here, they resisted a later influx of Hungarian immigrants who wanted to worship there in the Magyar language of their former oppressors.[16]

Inter-parish tensions existed as well. Pastors of territorial parishes that were predominantly Irish nevertheless resented the "poaching" of their non-Irish parishioners by national parishes. Catholic laity and priests accustomed to their own devotional practices were often less than appreciative of the devotions common in other ethnic groups, especially if such activities were performed in public where unsympathetic Protestants might see them: "Members of a German parish might have been shocked to observe 'tongue dragging' by women in Italian parishes, a feast day practice in which especially pious women dragged their tongues on the floor as they crawled or were carried down the aisle to the statue of the Madonna. Italians, in turn, might have been puzzled as to the religious significance of the huge, quasi-military pageants and processions held in German parishes to mark each of the major holy days."[17] Irish Catholics considered Italians' religious *feste* "rowdy," and were dismayed by their religious ignorance and lack of Mass attendance. In 1913, Archbishop James Quigley of Chicago complained that "the Italians who come from Southern Italy and Sicily are unexcelled in their ignorance of religion." A similar complaint was made in 1886 by the bishop of Burlington, Vermont, concerning the French Canadians in his diocese: they had, he said, "complete ignorance of religion . . . [and] knew not either confession or communion."[18]

Ethnic parish members also often engaged in conflict with the clergy and hierarchy. Some of the misunderstandings stemmed from cultural differences in respect for priests: the Irish, Germans, and Poles held the clergy and hierarchy in high esteem, while Italians were less impressed. The Irish hierarchy therefore stereotyped Italians "as anticlerical enemies of the papacy, unlikely to make good Catholic Americans."[19] A serious source of conflict erupted whenever bishops attempted to assign to an ethnic parish a pastor who was not of the parishioners' ethnicity. In 1884, for example, one New England bishop attempted to name an Irish pastor to a French Canadian parish: the resulting furor resulted in the parish being placed under a two-year interdict, until the bishop relented under Vatican pressure and allowed a French Canadian curate to assist the Irish pastor. Similar clashes between French Canadian parishes and Irish-American bishops occurred in Danielson, Connecticut (1894–96), Brookfield, Massachusetts (1899), Brunswick, Maine (1906), and Woonsocket, Rhode Island (1921–28).[20]

Ethnic parishes clashed with bishops over other issues as well. Having arrived first of all the ethnic groups, Irish Catholics dominated the hierarchy. Two-thirds of the American bishops in 1900 were of Irish descent, a proportion far exceeding the percentage of American Catholics with Irish backgrounds. In contrast, Germans, who comprised some 37 percent of all the Catholics in this country at that time, could boast of only 11 percent of the bishops.[21] Poles, Italians, and other ethnic groups had even less representation. "Justifiably, other ethnic groups have complained of Irish arrogance and insensitivity to their cultural needs and expressions."[22] Many Irish bishops wanted Catholics from other countries to assimilate to "normal" American Catholicism as quickly as possible and were less than sympathetic to the desires of French Canadians or Germans for preserving their own cultures. This led, one author charges, to "a sense of inferiority" among non-Irish Catholics.[23]

Conflicts also erupted over control of parish finances and governance. French Canadian, German, and Polish Catholic laity were accustomed to controlling the administration of their parishes: having collected the money to build and maintain them, they felt they should have a say over how they were run—including over who would be appointed pastor. The bishops, of course, resisted this "trusteeship" system and fought to wrest control from the parishioners. The struggles between French Canadians and the New England bishops mentioned above were fought at least partly over this issue.

Assimilation

According to the "melting pot" ideology common in the early twentieth century, the immigrants were expected to relinquish their former national identities and become Americans—if not in the first generation, at least in the second. Despite the fears of Protestant critics (and, for that matter, of some of the American Catholic hierarchy) that ethnic parishes and schools would prevent assimilation, the immigrants' institutions were, in fact, key factors in helping them adapt to middle-class American culture:

> The Irish parish in Chicago was a powerful force in transforming peas-
> ants into devout, disciplined urban dwellers. In the early years, it eased
> the burden of dislocation for immigrants and provided working-class
> Irish with models of middle-class behavior.[24]

Parish men's, women's, and youth societies also engaged in specific activities that fostered their members' Americanization. During World War I, for example, one parish's Young Ladies' Society helped America's soldiers by knitting socks and sweaters for them. The parishes "also introduced English plays, that further expanded their neighbors' horizons during the 1920s."[25] As Father Joseph Fitzpatrick, a Jesuit sociologist, noted, a strong community such as an ethnic parish was a key factor in the successful assimilation of nineteenth- and early twentieth-century immigrants.[26]

The gradual Americanization of the immigrants was reflected in the priests who served in the parishes. By 1926, 79 percent of the clergy in Chicago's Irish parishes, 68 percent of the clergy in its German parishes, and 53 percent of the clergy in its Polish parishes had been born in the United States.[27] To retain the younger generation, parishes began to offer Masses with English homilies, as well as parish missions, novenas, and other devotions entirely in English.

External events also accelerated the immigrants' assimilation into American culture. Protestants had become more suspicious of Catholics' loyalty after Pope Leo XIII's condemnation of "Americanism" in 1899, so American bishops balanced their fervent adherence to Rome on doctrinal matters with ostentatious displays of patriotism in other things:

> [Cardinal] Mundelein, for example, aligned himself with the "100 per-
> cent" attitude toward ethnic assimilation in America . . . . He believed
> that the transitional phase of immigrant accommodation in ethnic
> parishes had lasted long enough and that new immigrant groups should
> be nudged toward full assimilation.[28]

As soon as he arrived in Chicago, Mundelein appointed a new central school board that required all Catholic schools in his diocese to teach their pupils in English. In other parts of the country, it was the state legislatures that required English instruction. Whether because of ecclesiastical or state dictates, mandating English in the schools attenuated the ethnic culture of the immigrants' children and grandchildren. An additional national event that particularly influenced German Americans' assimilation was World War I. Anti-German patriotic fervor caused many German-language clubs, newspapers, and other groups to close, and many formerly German-language schools to switch to English.

Another external factor that encouraged assimilation was the sequential replacement of ethnic groups in urban neighborhoods. As Polish immigrants moved into Irish areas of a city, for example, they did not attend the Irish (territorial) parishes. Instead, they constructed their own churches—often only a block or two away. In Chicago, they built their St. Mary of the Angels Church and its school complex on an entire city block, "practically in the shadow of" the Irish Annunciation Church. "Saint Mary of the Angels soon became the center of a flourishing Polish neighborhood. The effect on Annunciation parish was immediate: church membership and school enrollment declined dramatically as Polish newcomers displaced older Irish residents."[29] Most of the Irish had been renters rather than homeowners, so it was easy for them simply to leave. When they did, they tended to move to outlying, predominantly Protestant, neighborhoods instead of reconstituting an Irish-American "ethnic village" elsewhere. This dispersion necessarily affected the "Irishness" of their Catholicity. "By 1920, a large segment of the Chicago Irish population had repudiated an ethnic identity in favor of a strictly Catholic identity,"[30] naming their fraternal organization the Knights of Columbus, for example, rather than the Knights of Columbanus as was current in Ireland. Another force for assimilation was intermarriage: third-generation Irish, Germans, and (later) Italians increasingly married across ethnic lines.

Immigrant Catholics Today

To what extent is this pattern—group migration to specific parts of the country, initial concentration in ethnic parishes, tensions and conflicts with previous immigrants, and gradual assimilation—prevalent today? According to a 2013 survey, the most common ancestry now cited by Catholic adults under age 65 is Mexican (19 percent). Mexican and Mexican-American Catholics are joined by Hispanic immigrants from other Latin American countries and the Caribbean, as well as by Puerto Ricans (who are US citizens by definition), and by the Hispanos and Chicanos of the Southwestern United States, whose ancestors have lived in this country longer than most Anglo Americans. Hispanics count for 71 percent of the growth in the US Catholic population since 1960.[31] Overall, 38 percent of US Catholic adults under the age of 65 claim a Hispanic or Latino ethnic identity. Among the youngest generation of Catholic adults—those in their twenties—the percentage exceeds 50 percent.[32]

As with earlier immigrant groups, Hispanics are concentrated in particular parts of the United States. Most Mexican and Central American immigrants tend to reside in the southwestern states of California, Arizona, New Mexico, Texas, and Colorado, but growing populations can also be found in North Carolina, Georgia, Arkansas, Florida, and Kansas, as well as in Chicago, Detroit, and other urban areas. More than 500,000 Puerto Ricans came to New York City between 1946 and 1964; they now comprise "the largest single ethnic group in the city boroughs of the Archdiocese of New York," and 41 percent of the Catholics in the entire Archdiocese.[33]

In addition to Hispanic/Latino and non-Hispanic white Catholics, the church in this country also includes almost three million Filipino, Korean, Indian, and other Catholics from Asia and the Pacific islands (4 percent of the total number of Catholics in this country), and over two million African American, African, and Afro-Caribbean Catholics (3 percent of the total). While their percentages may seem small, these populations, too, are often concentrated in a few dioceses. Most Asian-American Catholics live in the San Francisco and Los Angeles areas of California, along the New York-Washington corridor, in Chicago and Seattle, and along the Gulf Coast. African American Catholics, African immigrant Catholics, and Afro-Caribbean Catholics can be found in the large urban areas of the Northeast and Midwest, in the urban and rural South, and along the Pacific Coast in Los Angeles, San Francisco, and Seattle. A sizeable population of Afro-Caribbean Catholics can also be found in South Florida and in the New York City area.

Have these new concentrations of Catholic immigrants had the same church experiences as previous groups? While there have been some similarities, there have also been many differences. To begin with, Hispanic immigrants have usually not had specific parishes constructed for them. The 1918 codification of Canon Law required special permission before immigrants could construct their own parishes, that twentieth-century bishops were less willing to grant: "Therefore, when Spanish-speaking newcomers arrived from Mexico, the Catholic Church in Chicago did not welcome them as openly as it had previous immigrants from Europe."[34] Cardinal Mundelein did reluctantly authorize two national parishes and one storefront mission church for Mexicans, but

> this fell far short of meeting the religious needs of the immigrant com-
> munity. In some ways the existence of a few national parishes made the
> religious status of Mexican Catholics more ambiguous. When Mexican
> parents found their way to the nearest Catholic church to arrange a
> baptism for their child, the English-speaking pastor often told them
> to "go to the Mexican parish," that might be miles away in a strange
> neighborhood.[35]

In other areas, such as New York City, a single "Spanish parish" was founded to serve all Catholics speaking that language—some twenty different ethnic groups. This often reduced the sense of ownership and the feeling of being "at home" in what was really an amalgam of different cultures.[36]

Like the Italians before them, Mexicans and other Hispanic migrants had practiced a largely home-based and folk version of lay Catholicism in their home countries. Religion was infused into the entirety of their daily lives:

> Religion in that mountain town of my childhood was part of daily life
> despite the fact that some of us saw the priest and visited the town
> church sparingly. The day would always begin with my mother opening
> up the windows and doors and proclaiming: "May God's grace enter
> upon this house and those therein and may it remain with us always."
> When we left home to help in the fields or go to school, we always
> asked for a blessing from our parents. The same was done upon return-
> ing . . . . A statue or an icon of the Blessed Mother made the rounds
> of the dwellings of the mountain town, where it was kept overnight.
> There was a prayer to greet the statue and a prayer to take leave of it.
> We prayed the holy rosary promptly after sunset every night, and no
> one in the family was excused from this obligation.[37]

Home rituals such as these were, in some cultures, supplemented by lay-led church activities. People in many parts of Latin America, especially in the rural areas, had been "thinly pastored" since the early 1800s. Missionaries in the twentieth century, therefore, attempted to train lay leaders for the local churches that the priests could visit only rarely. In Guatemala, for example, "The lay leaders who went through the Maryknoll training programs began a tradition of initiative and self-reliance in church matters that is still operative today. Each village has a prayer leader, teachers for adult religious education, and a choir."[38] Immigrants who were used to actively creating their own religious practices, whether at home or in church, were not attracted to the more passive, "church-on-Sunday" Catholicism practiced in many North American parishes.[39]

Accustomed to organizing and leading their own religious rituals, Hispanic immigrants did not bring their own clergy with them when they came, as the Germans, Poles, Irish, and French Canadians had done. The American hierarchy, therefore, needed actively to lure the new arrivals into a parish-centered and clergy-run Catholicism. This had been one of the reasons for founding national parishes in the past:

> when the Italians came to Chicago, the archdiocese actively promoted the formation of national parishes and subsidized them indefinitely. It did not leave them wandering about looking for a parish community that would welcome them, as it did [later] with the Mexicans and Puerto Ricans. Preoccupied with suburban growth, Catholic authorities after World War II forgot that the ethnic parish was a tried and true institution of immigrant adjustment and neglected to promote it among the Spanish-speaking.[40]

By the 1950s and 60s, it was assumed that simply allowing the new migrants to attend the local parish and training the already-existing English-speaking pastors and parish staff to accommodate to their needs would insure that Hispanics "would not be ecclesiastically isolated but involved immediately in the life of the local parish."[41]

In practice, this was less successful. Many pastors and parish staff resisted learning a new language and culture. There was also a tendency to assume that all immigrants from Latin America and the Caribbean shared the same "Hispanic" culture. This was, and is, not the case: Maya Catholics from Guatemala, for example, do not necessarily even speak Spanish, and the root paradigms of their culture are profoundly different from other Latin Americans.[42] Attempts to include all Latin American cultural groups in a single parish, or in a single "Hispanic" parade or fiesta, often ended by alienating all of them.[43] Additionally, by the time that many Hispanics arrived in the urban areas of the Northeast and Midwest, Catholic schools were either closing or becoming too expensive for them to afford to send their children there. Thus, Hispanics were often denied the opportunity for Catholic schools to help them integrate their own cultural versions of Catholic identity with the American version.

In spite of these initial difficulties, many parishes in the United States today do have substantial Hispanic populations, while others serve various

Asian or African groups. In 2013, the United States Conference of Catholic Bishops commissioned the Center for Applied Research in the Apostolate (CARA) to conduct a study of the cultural and ethnic diversity of Catholics in this country. In addition to counting the number and percentage of Catholics self-identifying as belonging to a particular ethnic group, the study also attempted to count how many parishes were serving them. CARA identified a total of 6,332 parishes that were known to serve one or more racial, ethnic, cultural, and/or linguistic groups—35.9 percent of all the parishes in the United States.[44] Of these 6,332 parishes, 72 percent serve Hispanic/Latino Catholics; 13 percent serve Asian or Pacific Islander Catholics; and 2 percent serve Native American Catholics. The remaining 13 percent (831 parishes) continue to serve older European ethnic groups such as Italians, Poles, or Ukrainians.

Table 1.2 Parishes Offering Services for Ethnic Groups, 2010				
Ethnic Group	Number of Parishes	% of Total Number of Parishes	Number of Adherents	% of Total Number of Adherents
Hispanic/Latino	4,544	25.8%	29,731,302	38%
Asian, total	463	2.7%	2,905,925	4.0%
Filippino	NA	NA	2,200,000	2.8%
Vietnamese	232	1.3%	483,600	0.6%
Korean	130	0.7%	199,698	0.2%
Indian	NA	NA	146,400	0.2%
Native American	101	0.6%	536,601	0.7%
Sub-Saharan African	NA	NA	330,000	0.4%
European (Italian, Polish, etc.)	831	4.7%	NA	NA
Percentage of Ethnic Parishes		35.9%		
Total # of Catholic Parishes/Adherents	17,638		78,240,268	

Source: Mark Gray, Melissa Cidade, Mary Gautier, and Thomas Gaunt, SJ. "Cultural Diversity in the Catholic Church in the United States," Center for Applied Research in the Apostolate (CARA), Georgetown University, 2013, 11.

With the exception of this last 14 percent, however, the majority of today's ethnic parishes were not specifically established to serve the particular ethnic population that currently attends them. Bishops have been reluctant to approve new ethnic parishes today, assuming that the eventual assimilation of the founding ethnic group's children would render such parishes superfluous. No bishop wants to be saddled with another crop of overlapping churches, each holding a remnant of elderly immigrant parishioners:

> [Cardinal] Spellman generally worried about the wisdom of retaining nationality parishes, not only because they seemed to retard assimilation and to perpetuate the image of the church as a foreign institution, but also because they were so temporary. By the third generation, the English-speaking grandchildren of German, Slavic, and Italian immigrants were heading for the suburbs, leaving behind huge nationality churches with a few dozen elderly members . . . . Why not move instead to integrated, mixed parishes serving elderly immigrants of an earlier generation as well as the young immigrants of the latest group?[45]

Few parishes today, therefore, have been specifically founded for a particular ethnic group. Those few that were so founded are often not full-fledged parishes but rather "centers" or missions—a subordinate status that one Korean-American priest decries: "being labeled something other than actual parishes suppress[es] the necessary and healthy development as a U.S. immigrant and ethnic church, thus stifling any contribution to the universal Church."[46] This lack of their "own" parish has been seen by critics as a crippling deficiency:

> Today, as in the past, people migrating to the United States bring their religions with them, and gathering religiously is one of the ways they make a life here. Their religious identities often (but not always) mean more to them away from home, in their diaspora, then they did before, and those identities undergo more or less modification as the years pass.[47]

The inability to found, and to take subsequent responsibility for, their "own" parish hampers today's immigrants in the preservation of their own culture, as well as in their smooth adaptation to Catholicism as practiced in this country. Less than 10 percent of the pastoral leaders surveyed in 2014 by Boston College's School of Theology and Ministry said that Hispanic parishioners are "fully" integrated into their parishes.[48]

For better or for worse, the majority of today's Hispanic, Asian, and African immigrants attend parishes with other ethnic groups. This means that the average "Catholics in the pew," of all races and ethnicities, are confronted with these cultural differences much more intensively than Catholics experienced in the nineteenth century, when they attended separate, monoethnic parishes. This could open the door for more misunderstanding and conflicts, but it could also provide a unique and precious opportunity for enriching the Catholic (that, after all, means "universal") identities and practices of all involved. For this to happen, however, we need to understand how the deeper dimensions of culture—its value and cognitive dimensions as well as its material and behavioral ones—operate to shape Catholic belief and practice. This is the task of the next chapter.

2

Catholicism through Ethnic Eyes

"The history of the Church shows that Christianity does not have simply
one cultural expression, but rather . . . it will also reflect the different
faces of the cultures and peoples in which it is received and takes root."

— Pope Francis, *Evangelii Gaudium* 116

What does it mean for a religion to have different cultural expressions?
Using the fourfold characterization of culture outlined in the introduction,
this chapter will explore some of the cognitive, behavioral, value, and material
aspects of Catholic cultures, as these aspects are enacted and expressed by the
various ethnic groups that populate our parishes today. Of course, ethnicity is
not the only dimension along which Catholic cultures can vary. The second
part of this book will look at generational cultures in Catholicism as well. In
addition to ethnicity and generation, there are also different class, urban/rural,
and gender cultures among Catholics. But in this chapter, we will examine
how our faith is reflected in and through the lives of the different ethnic
groups that make up the Catholic Church in the United States. In much
the same way as in the story of the blind men who each tried to describe an
elephant by feeling a different part of it, these various cultural expressions,
while separately incomplete and partial, together enrich our understanding
of the full richness of Catholicism today.

Cognitive Culture

At the deepest level, the cognitive and value dimensions of culture are
religious in nature because they define for us what reality *is* and what *matters most* in it. These cognitive and value dimensions are the root paradigms
that structure our lives, to the point that it never occurs to us even to imagine other ways of thinking. If we should come upon a person or group of

people who do think or act differently, we may find them to be literally incomprehensible.

The root paradigms of our cognitive culture tell us who God is and what is the ultimate meaning of human life. They give us answers to questions like the ones listed below, answers at such a subconscious level that it usually does not even occur to us to ask the questions.

- Is the Divinity benign and forgiving, or a stern judge? Closely and personally involved in our daily lives, or distant and only to be approached through intermediaries? If the latter, who are the appropriate intermediaries—one's personal patron saint, a local holy person, or the parish priest?

- Is there a basic balance to things? Is it a sign of God's favor if we are currently successful, or is our present success a deeply unsettling omen that we will suffer some future misfortune in order to balance things?

- What determines our destinies: Luck? Fate? God's will? Our family or class background? Or our own initiative?

- Are human beings perfectible? Are lapses like a premarital pregnancy or a weekend drinking binge the understandable and even expected results of human frailty? Or are such actions a reprehensible deviation from normal and expected behavior?

- What about priests? Are they holier, wiser, or more in touch with the divine? Or is there something odd and suspicious about some guy who isn't married?

- Were people better in the old days? Is the world going to hell in a handbasket? Can we stop it from doing so?

- Are outsiders for us or against us? Is there a "war against religion" going on? Who is waging it? Are they likely to win?

Questions like these, that we rarely even bother to articulate because we take their answers so thoroughly for granted, have obvious religious implications. To the extent that different ethnic cultures in our parishes assume different answers to them, however, we will find it hard to understand each other. As examples of differences in cognitive culture between different ethnic groups of Catholics, we might cite the following:

- *Relating to God and the saints.* While both Anglo and Hispanic Catholics pray to Mary and the saints, it is also common for them to pray directly to God or Jesus. Both sometimes make a promise (*promesas*) to God or a saint, either to do something (go to Mass, visit a shrine) or to give up something (smoking, ice cream) if their prayer is granted. But they accept the fact that "Sometimes God says no." Haitian Catholics, however, are less inclined to pray to God directly and prefer to strike a bargain with a saint by telling that saint what they want and what they will give in return. "If one saint does not give us what we want, we may berate it, argue with it, and ultimately turn to a different saint with the same wish. Just as we can punish them by turning away, they can punish us if we do not live up to our promise . . . . Making promises to the saint is tricky: 'Watch out, because if you promise something to them and then you forget, you're in trouble.'"[1] A spurned and vengeful saint may become angry and cause you to fall and break your leg, or to lose your job, or to develop cancer or some other disease.

• *Balance, fate:* Americans, including Anglo American Catholics, are likely to assume that an individual determines his or her own fate, and that success in this life is not only possible but expected. For rural Mexicans, in contrast, life is a precarious balance of opposites: pain and pleasure, health and illness, life and death. "At the top of this world, making sure that all suffering was eventually relieved and all prosperity eventually humbled, was God. In everyone's life, achieving a harmony between extremes was the only way of surviving."[2] In this traditional, rural culture, striving to surpass the other members of one's community in anything, including religiosity, was disruptive of this harmony. A contrasting attitude is expressed in Koreans' feelings of *han*, a discontent that leads them constantly to feel inferior because they *haven't* been successful enough. Rather than being at peace in their relationship with God, Korean and Korean-American Catholics are constantly comparing—unfavorably—their own personal spiritual progress with that of others.[3] Korean Catholics, one author notes, are driven by their *han* to ascribe to a "militaristic model" of devotion. "Being told how to pray and act in church and the world becomes a powerful measuring stick," and the majority of Korean Catholic immigrants attend weekly Legion of Mary meetings where all members must report to the group how many rosaries, Masses, and service hours they offered in the preceding week.[4]

• *The status of priests and laity:* Americans have a strong belief in the equality of all persons, a belief that is reflected in American Catholics' interpretation of the church as a People of God in which all, laity as well as priests and religious, are equally called to holiness. In contrast, Asian immigrant Catholics are more influenced by Confucian tenets of filial piety and, for them, "the church literally represents God's family, a household on earth, more so than perhaps anywhere else. Thus, bishops and priests enjoy the place of honor as the head of this particular household."[5] At the opposite extreme, a famous study of Italian immigrant Catholics at the turn of the last century noted that one's family, not the church, was the center of religious and moral life. There was intense suspicion of anyone who was not a member of a family—including, most especially, celibate diocesan priests.[6] Celibacy was assumed to be impossible for any man, and priests were commonly thought to be secretly having sexual relations with somebody—possibly even one's own wife or daughters. This anticlerical suspicion has been documented in other folk cultures in Europe and Latin America.[7]

Basic underlying assumptions such as these form the ground or basis for all of our thinking about God and for our relationship(s) with the Divine. We naturally assume that our own cognitive culture is correct and that others are being deliberately obtuse if they do not recognize this. Thus, for example, missionaries in former days attempted to remold the spiritual practices of Guatemalan Maya Catholics—praying to the four directions, pouring rum on the ground for the mountain spirits, consulting a diviner before naming a baby—to the standard Westernized model.[8] Similarly, missionaries to East Asia tried to extirpate "ancestor worship." But no image of God, including the Western Catholic one, can possibly capture the full essence of the Divine. All have unique insights and unique blind spots. Becoming aware of how other cognitive cultures answer questions about the ultimate meaning and purpose of reality will both challenge and enrich our own version of Catholicism.

Cultural Values

The root paradigms of a culture also include what its members value as good, beautiful, and/or desirable. Again, these value aspects are unquestioned by those who hold them, no matter how odd they may appear to others. In contrast to the "taken-for-grantedness" of cognitive culture, however, human beings have long been aware that there are differences in cultural values, even if they do not agree with them. A cursory search of Wikipedia finds proverbs similar to the English saying, "There is no accounting for taste," in twenty-one different languages, from Armenian to Turkish. Also unlike the cognitive aspects of culture, some of a culture's value aspects do change over time, as anyone looking at the clothing styles and popular music of the 1890s—or even of the 1970s—can certainly attest. The value dimension of culture mandates specific behaviors that must be engaged in, or material items that must be displayed, in order to show that one is adhering to the correct values. Some of the questions that the value dimension of culture answers for us are the following:

- *Priorities:* Which is the most important goal in our lives, to which all else must be subordinated: Family solidarity? Financial success? Status in one's society? The honor of the family's men? Of its women?

  - *Associated Behaviors*: What must a man/woman/child do in order to safeguard family solidarity? What kinds of activities must be engaged in—or avoided—in order to safeguard women's honor?

  - *Material culture*: What visible goods must be purchased and displayed to broadcast one's financial success or social status? To show that one is an appropriately modest wife?

- What are the most *desirable personal characteristics* for women—or men, or the young, or the old—to have? Assertiveness? Humility? Pugnaciousness? Physical strength? Beauty? Intelligence? What are the absolutely *un*desirable characteristics?

  - What specific *behaviors* indicate these personal characteristics? How does a "real man" walk, talk, dress? How does a "good girl" behave?

  - *Material culture*: What kind(s) of items indicate that one is not to be "messed with" by outsiders? That one is intelligent? What items would be make their possessor a laughing stock?

- *What is beautiful or ugly*: This includes visual beauty as well as what is thought beautiful in music, delicious in food, etc.

  - *Behaviors*: What is the ideal body type for a man/woman to have? What is the appropriate way to stand or walk? What style of language and tone of voice should be used by a man? By a woman?

  - *Material culture*: What is the current fashion in dress? In music? In architecture and art? What is out-of-date or ugly?

- The *emotional "tone"* attached to situations, objects, words, concepts. Is it a compliment or a put-down to call someone a "geek"? Or a "hipster"? Or a "feminist"?

- *Behaviors:* Is an actor smoking a cigarette in a film radiating high status and sophistication, or betraying a low-status or working-class background? What about a father washing the dishes or diapering the baby—is he "henpecked" or an involved parent?
- *Material culture*: What message does wearing polyester slacks convey? Or torn jeans? Would these items of apparel have conveyed the same message in the 1950s that they do now?

As with differences in cognitive culture, differences in cultural values and their resulting behaviors can impact how Catholicism is lived in a given ethnic group. On the most obvious level, they affect the kinds of worship spaces a group constructs or adapts, and the kinds of ritual activities performed there. Nineteenth-century German Catholics took pride in "elaborate ceremonies and pageantry," with skilled choirs and musicians as well as *lustige Gesang* ("hearty singing") by the congregation.[9] Polish immigrants, too—even in poor parishes—constructed ornate churches. Other ethnic groups, in contrast, prefer to perform devotional rituals at their household shrines rather than in church. Familiar music, singing, incense, art, and rituals all serve to awaken and intensify the feeling of a sacred time and space and to lead the participants into prayer. This is why such bitter controversies can arise between parish groups when a specific style of music or type of behavior is deeply meaningful to one side and off-putting to the other. Maya Catholics from Guatemala play slow and plaintive marimba music—very differently from the way the instrument is played in Mexico—in their worship services. One author notes that the Maya disagree about how "Latino" their marimba music can be allowed to become in order to appeal to other Hispanic groups and the general public and yet not lose "its mystical significance as Indian cultural property."[10]

Misunderstandings arise when one ethnic group's religious icons or practices are repellent to another group. Early "Anglo" missionary sisters in Santa Fe in 1906 were appalled by the statuary in one local Mexican shrine:

The first room we entered looked like a chapel . . . on the wall back of it was a very large crucifix. The figure was all covered but we raised the cover and O! such a sight! The face of the image was awful and the whole figure was covered with daubs of red paint which made a very realistic representation of blood . . . . Any number of ugly little statues were hanging on the wall but the gem of the whole collection was the statue or skeleton which represented "death.". . . The whole figure . . .

was enveloped in a black cloak which was drawn up over the head and face leaving only the horrible jaw and eyeless sockets visible.[11]

The very statues and decorations that inspired awe and devotion in one Catholic culture were considered bizarre and frightening by the members of another.

Differences in cultural values affect how different ethnic cultures live Catholicism in US parishes today. One author noted that, for her Puerto Rican ethnic group, the church was "the center of a living community. Since many of the parishioners were related by blood, marriage or friendship, it also functioned as an extended family. It was a place to worship and celebrate religious events, but it was also where parishioners could see and speak in their own language to cousins, aunts, uncles, and friends."[12] The high priority placed by Hispanic cultures on family solidarity means that they will bring their small children to Mass—even to an Easter Vigil service at 10:00 or 11:00 p.m.—to the occasional consternation of Anglo parishioners who find the children's behavior disruptive. ("Why aren't these kids at home in bed?") The Hispanic parishioners, in contrast, would be just as scandalized if they *weren't* allowed to bring their children.

Both for Hispanic and for some East Asian Catholic immigrants, Sunday church is "not a one-hour reality." After Mass is the time for eating together: "sharing a meal together at the Eucharistic table as well as in the dining hall afterward."[13] This can cause resentment: Diaz-Stevens quotes Anglo parishioners who complained that the Hispanic parishioners "are too loud; they do not seem to know that Holy Mass is not a fiesta," and that they were crowding the narthex and parking lot when the Anglos were trying to get in to *their* Mass. Fortunately, however, these critics were balanced by others who commented on "the friendliness of the Spanish speaking." There were even cases where English-speaking members attended the Hispanic Mass and joined one of their parish societies because they found the worship services more alive and participative.[14]

In addition to cultural differences in their formal worship at Mass, most of the various Catholic ethnic groups that have migrated here also engaged in other religious activities such as pilgrimages, festivals, parades, and home-based worship. Most of these are organized and run by lay groups, who jealously guard them from interference by the ordained clergy. While the hierarchy and priests who ministered to Harlem's Italians in the early twentieth century opposed spending so much time and money on elaborate processions for the feast—to say nothing of the drinking and partying that accompanied it—"it was especially on occasions such as these that the parish was becoming the point of reference for the entire ethnic community."[15] The procession on the feast of Our Lady of Mount Carmel, July 16, "grew to be a major ritual marker in Italian New York, helping Italians forge an American identity based largely on their Catholicism."[16] Similar observations have been made of the Puerto Rican *Fiesta de San Juan*, St. Patrick's Day parades among Irish Americans, and Mexican American pilgrimages to Chimayo.[17] At times, however, efforts have been made to ban rituals that mainstream Catholics found offensive: the Good Friday practices of the Penitente fraternities of the Southwest, for example.

One of the reasons for objecting to these extra-liturgical expressions of ethnic devotion is, of course, because they contain elements of whatever previous religion the immigrants practiced prior to their conversion to Catholicism—elements that, after several centuries, have been thoroughly incorporated into that culture's version of Catholic practice. The devotions at Chimayo contain elements of Native American mythology; Our Lady of Guadalupe appeared on the same site an Aztec goddess had formerly inhabited, and in clothing reminiscent of a (pregnant) Aztec princess. New York's Haitians follow Vodou practices of leaving money and food for the spirits in Catholic churches, and sprinkle Florida Water, a cologne used in Vodou rituals. Maya immigrants follow the sacred calendar of their ancestors, "which consists of two intertwined cycles of named and numbered days, each with its own patron spirit, assigned prayer intentions, and probable luck."[18] The Maya have a special festival and dance at the beginning of their year because they believe that the new cycle of crops and children needs to be danced in.[19] More assimilated North American Catholics may look askance at these "pagan" remnants, forgetting the pagan origins of their own religious practices: Christmas trees, the immersion of the Easter candle in the baptismal font on Holy Saturday, and so on.[20] As one author has noted, there is no "pure" Catholicism—or "pure" any religion, for that matter. We are all "hybrids" whose sacred stories contain elements borrowed from other faiths.[21]

Finally, the various ethnic groups that make up the American Catholic Church also have differing cultural values regarding the proper and expected roles for men and women. These value differences, too, can impact how a given ethnic group expresses its Catholic practice in this country. In numerous cultures, churchgoing is primarily a female activity. Expecting men to attend Sunday Mass—even minimally by coming late, standing in the back of the church, and leaving early—is expecting them to go against a deeply-ingrained cultural norm on how "real men" are supposed to behave. The ethnic group's various parades and festivals, too, are often events in which male gender roles were acted out—to the consternation of the clergy:

> [Nineteenth-century St. Patrick's Day parades] demonstrated the traditional Irish male preference for infrequent enthusiastic displays of piety and patriotism, ritualized expressions of male bonding, and a willingness to accept poverty tomorrow for a grand time today . . . Few official Catholic rituals were connected with them, only pietistic expressions. The festivities included drinking, flourishes of colorfully dressed marchers, speeches, and general rabble-rousing.[22]

Women's expected gender roles will also impact the way they express their Catholic identity in this country. In some cultures, women are expected to be humble and retiring, which will make it difficult to persuade them to become involved in parish activities. At the same time, women may be expected to be the primary person in charge of home-based devotions: making and maintaining the home altars, preparing food for the ritual meals, and offering the prayers to the altar's various saints. Such home services have been documented for Haitians, Filipinos, Koreans, and most Hispanic groups.[23] For both men and women, home services are a way for the laity to exercise control over their own spiritual practice and to maintain traditional religious practices that do not necessarily correspond to mainstream Catholicism.

Caveats

While it may be true, as Pope Francis said, that Christianity must reflect "the different faces of the cultures and peoples in which it is received and takes root," this is often problematic in the daily life of most parishes and dioceses. It is often difficult to discern which elements of a given ethnic culture are valuable for all parishioners to learn from and which elements should be challenged and corrected. Should parishes allow *quinceanera* celebrations that are more elaborate than sacramental marriages? What about having women serve on the parish council if the men object?

Still another problem stems from the phenomenon of "supertribalization." Many immigrant groups—the Germans and Italians, for example—did not arrive here with a "German" or "Italian" national identity. Instead, they identified with a home village or province. It was only when they were labeled "German" or "Italian" (or, more likely, "Kraut" or "Wop") by other Americans that they began to think of themselves as having this national identity. As one calypso song, describing the amalgamation of various Caribbean islanders into a common "West Indian" ethnicity, put it:

> You can be from St. Cleo or John John,
> In New York, all that done!
> They haven't to know who is who,
> New York equalize you![24]

In the same way, Spanish-speaking Catholic immigrants from Mexico, Central America, Cuba, and other countries (to say nothing of Puerto Ricans, Chicano/as, Hispanos/as and others who have been US citizens for generations) may all be lumped together into one large category of "Hispanics" and assumed to have the same cultural variant of Catholic practice. As has already been noted for the Maya immigrants from Guatemala, this is not true. Similarly, Filipino, Korean, Chinese, Hmong, and Vietnamese Catholics (and even Indian and Pakistani Catholics) may all be amalgamated into one "Asian and Pacific islander" category. West Indian and Western African immigrants may struggle to keep from being identified as African Americans—to the point, sometimes, of sending their children to "accent schools" to acquire the accent of their parents' home country. When is super-tribalization empowering, as it was for New York's West Indian community, and when does it ignore important differences?

Answering this question becomes even more difficult when we realize that a given ethnic group itself may be divided on the issue. The older generation's members may still prefer to identify with their home state of Jalisco, Chihuahua, or Oaxaca while the second generation self-identifies simply as "Mexican-American" or even as "Hispanic," thus blurring distinctions that were significant to their parents. There are no right or wrong answers to this dilemma, and the answers are continually changing. "Immigrants and their children pick, borrow, retain, and create distinctive cultural forms. People navigate across cultural boundaries as well as make conscious decisions in the production of culture."[25] Pastoral practices, too, will need to change in response.

Conclusion

This chapter has outlined a daunting task. Cognitive cultural differences in how parishioners from different ethnic backgrounds conceive of God's relationship to humankind, value differences in their preferred worship styles, music, and places, behavioral differences in the way they participate at Mass or in their gender roles—all may seem impossibly difficult to accommodate in a single parish. Add in the differences that occur within each ethnic group as its original members are replaced by their Americanized children or by newer migrants, and parish ministers may be tempted simply to throw up their hands in despair.

But as Pope Francis has said, it is precisely this ongoing production of their culture, as each ethnic group adapts to its changing circumstances, that makes them "active collective subjects or agents of evangelization." Their popular piety is "a true expression of the spontaneous missionary activity of the People of God."[26] Over fifty years ago, the director of the New York Archdiocese's Office of Spanish American Catholic Action made a similar point:

> [Msgr. Robert] Fox made Puerto Rican culture into a kind of sacrament; it was to be venerated as a sign of something sacred. Those who recognized the human values of Puerto Rican customs and traditions were placed in the presence of God's work among the poor of this earth. According to Fox's vision, the Puerto Ricans did not need evangelization from the official Church, because their own rich religious culture had kept them close to Catholicism.[27]

All cultures are sacred; they are the way in which a given group of people, led by the Spirit, reflect the face of God—partially and incompletely, it is true, but nevertheless in a way that is unique. "Each portion of the People of God, by translating the gift of God into its own life and in accordance with its own genius, bears witness to the faith it has received and enriches it with new and eloquent expressions."[28] Each local church is called to promote and deepen "the never ending process of inculturation."[29]

3

Welcoming Ethnic Cultures

"[You] . . . have put on the new self, which is being renewed . . . in the image of its creator. Here there is not Greek and Jew, circumcision and uncircumcision, barbarian, Scythian, slave, free; but Christ is all and in all."
—Colossians 3:10-11

Recent studies have shown that Catholic parishes contain the most ethnically diverse congregations of all Christian denominations in the United States.[1] And they are becoming even more diverse: in 2000, 22 percent of all Catholic parishes in the United States were shared by at least two culturally-diverse communities, while in 2010, that percentage had risen to 33 percent.[2] More and more, both the pastoral staff and the members of our parishes must confront the recurrent dilemmas of welcoming multiple cultures. In the nineteenth century, bishops, pastors, and laity responded to these dilemmas by establishing separate parish churches for each immigrant group. There were pros and cons to this policy: on the one hand, historians and sociologists have found that it helped the immigrants adapt to American culture in a more gradual and less-disruptive way, while in the process giving legitimacy and recognition to their own cultural expressions of Catholicism. On the other hand, these ethnic parishes were often "ghettoized" and isolated from ecclesial power networks that continued to be dominated by Irish and Irish-American prelates. Sometimes, as in the case of the Polish National Church, separatist tendencies led to actual schisms. And the more that ethnic parishes were successful in preserving the particular culture of Catholicism that they had brought from the old country, the less successful they were in retaining the loyalty of the second and third generation. Elderly founding members resisted changes in the language of the sermons and devotions, in the expectations of proper male and female behavior in church and elsewhere, and in the number of "respectable" activities for parish fraternities. Their children and grandchildren, tired of fighting their elders' "old-fashioned" ways, decamped to English-speaking parishes—or even left Catholicism altogether.

Today, in contrast, several nationalities may share the same parish: a 2002 survey of immigrant faith communities in the Washington, DC, archdiocese showed that 73 percent of Catholic immigrant faith communities were part of larger, multiethnic, parishes, while only 27 percent worshipped in parishes for a single ethnicity.[3] But another recent survey found that Hispanics were, for the most part, only minimally integrated into the larger life of these parishes.[4]

In considering the pros and cons of these two ways of dealing with diverse ethnic groups, the church is replicating a recurring dilemma that has also faced the larger American society: choosing between assimilation and pluralism. In theory, assimilation refers to the "melting pot" image of America: immigrants from all the cultures of the world are "melted down" into one American culture, each contributing his or her cultural bit to enrich the mix, but overall becoming something new. In practice, however, assimilation really means "Anglo-Conformity." Immigrants are expected to relinquish their language, as well as their culturally-distinct family patterns, their accepted gender roles, their ways of raising children, and their myriad other "odd" customs, in order to become "real Americans." If they are allowed to keep anything of their old way of life, it will be something minor and innocuous—a particular ethnic food or a quaint festival, for example—as long as it is not *too* different.[5] The rest of American society might even adopt one of the immigrants' foods or customs: salsa has replaced catsup as the most popular American condiment, and all sorts of non-Irish people celebrate St. Patrick's Day. But, for the most part, immigrants to the United States are expected to relinquish their original culture. Canadians, in contrast, refer to the metaphor of a "Salad Bowl" as a model for their more pluralistic national policy. Immigrants to Canada are not as pressured to give up their distinctive cultures. Each element of the Canadian "tossed salad" retains its original identity, while it adds to the tastiness of the whole.

Both of these two policies have positive and negative implications. Assimilation—to say nothing of Anglo-Conformity—means the destruction of the group's original culture. In my classes on Race and Ethnic Relations, I often hand out a poem that appeared in the university's student newspaper a few years ago. The poem envisioned an idyllic future America in which race would vanish. I point out that, if such an America ever did come about and race really didn't matter, then 88 percent of all African Americans would marry white people, and so would 88 percent of *their* children. In two generations, African Americans would no longer exist—they would be assimilated. I then ask the African Americans in the class if something would be lost. I have yet to have a single African American student who did not agree that, yes, something very precious would indeed be lost—their culture. This, of course, is precisely what did happen to many of the white immigrant groups that arrived here in the nineteenth century. Their children and grandchildren were no longer Germans, Poles, Italians, etc.—they were Americans. They had lost their original ethnic identity; they had become strangers to their grandparents and great-grandparents, if these older generations were still around to observe them.

From a more positive viewpoint, however, assimilation does help to maintain a nation's unity and identity. To a certain extent, more explicitly pluralistic Canada does not have as uniform a national identity as its neighbor to the south. A Canadian radio station once had a contest for its listeners to come up with a slogan to parallel "As American as apple pie." The winner was "As Canadian as possible under the circumstances." Canada is an example of a (more or less) successful pluralism.[6] But pluralism as a national policy, while a commendable way of preserving the beauties of each component culture in a country, can also have disastrous results if it is not implemented with care and sensitivity. We have only to look at any number of countries, from the former Yugoslavia to present-day Iraq, to see the disastrous consequences of retaining or increasing pluralistic sentiments among various ethnic groups.

Intercultural Relations in Parishes

As more and more Catholic parishes have come to contain several different ethnic groups, it has become necessary to discern whether and how to welcome them into the same parish family. In 2007, the Catholic bishops of the United States listed cultural diversity as one of the top five priorities they wanted to address and so established a Committee on Cultural Diversity in the Church to develop guides for parishes and parish leaders. These guides were accordingly published in 2012 and 2013. Both note that there are six stages that the typical parish and its staff pass through when confronted by a new ethnic group within its boundaries:[7]

1. *Denial:* The pastor, staff, and congregation don't even notice the new group in the area. Immigrants from country X might be a problem elsewhere, they say, but not here.

2. *Defense:* Once the presence of the new ethnic group in the local area becomes too obvious to deny, there is a tendency to rationalize why its members don't, or shouldn't, come to *this* church. Often these rationalizations are motivated by negative stereotypes of the new group, or by a feeling that "they" will take over what "we" have built.

3. *Minimizing:* The pastor, staff, and congregation claim to welcome the newcomers but assume that they won't need to change anything about the way the parish currently operates. As the authors of a recent book put it, what they really mean is that all are welcome on *our* terms: if you dress like us, speak our language, like the same style church music we like, and worship in the same way we do.[8]

4. *Acceptance:* The parish establishes Sunday liturgies for the new group in its own language and perhaps provides space and facilities for their other activities as well. But it still functions as two parallel communities who rarely interact except to negotiate, more or less amicably, for facility space and Mass times.

5. *Adaptation:* The worship, catechetical, and other activities of the new group are more incorporated into the life of the parish. The pastor and staff develop some amount of intercultural competence (for example, they learn to speak the language of the new group). Both the new arrivals and the older members begin to speak of themselves as "we." But the new group still does not have full voice in parish policies or on parish decision-making committees.

6. *Integration:* At this stage, the pastor, the staff, and the leaders of both communities have a sense of ownership of the parish. They participate equally on decision-making committees, resources are shared equitably, and each group "move[s] quite naturally from one cultural framework to the other, adapting to different situations with ease and cultural accuracy."[9]

It is the transition between stage 4 and stage 5 that is tricky. True intercultural competence, the bishops' committee acknowledges, is the most difficult to achieve.[10] It requires being able to see situations (sometimes situations that the participants feel quite strongly about) from more than one perspective, and being able to understand another culture's different interpretations of reality. In other words, *it involves being open to a different cognitive culture than one's own*— precisely the dimension of culture that is the hardest even to notice and the hardest to change. The bishops' committee also noted that intercultural competence requires skills that not everyone has: the ability to speak more than one language and adapt one's own communication style and behavior to those of a different ethnic group, the ability to tolerate ambiguity, and attitudes such as empathy and openness to learning about another culture.[11] Note also that *both* groups, the established parishioners and the newcomers, have to be able to do this. Developing such a mindset and such skills is a work of years, if not decades.

It is therefore difficult to discern when it is best to encapsulate a given ethnic group in the parish into its own subcommunity so that the people can maintain their own cognitive, value, behavioral, and material cultures (Stage 4)—and when it is better to unite the various groups so that they can learn from, *and change*, each other (Stage 5). One Puerto Rican sociologist describes this dilemma in a New York parish:

> *Las misas de sotano*, as Masses in the lower church came to be referred to, served as a constant reminder that despite their Catholocity and United States citizenship, discrimination existed in the church. While Mass in the upper church was the definition of upward mobility in the context of church community, it also required abandoning the Spanish language in worship and Puerto Rican Catholic customs. The Puerto Ricans were conscious that as long as they practiced Puerto Rican Catholicism, they were stuck in the basement.[12]

Moving out of "the basement" without adequate preparation on both sides will mean either that the ethnic group will have to abandon its own way of worshipping, or that the "upstairs" church will be forced unwillingly to accept a different culture in their own worship. Either can be a recipe for conflict. Both the "basement" and the "upstairs" cultures will have to change, and change is difficult.

But refusing to change has its own perils. The "upstairs" church that refuses to change will gradually dwindle in membership, since it will be less and less attractive to new ethnic and generational cultures. The "basement" church that remains in the basement, retaining its original ethnic version of Catholicism, may lose its subsequent, more Americanized, generations. Second-generation Korean Americans, for example, often do not understand Korean well enough to follow a Sunday sermon delivered in that language. They prefer to attend Mass in English, while their elders prefer Mass in Korean. But if different generations attend different services, even in the same parish, this will violate another important Korean value: family unity.[13] Similarly, second-generation immigrant women may desire more involvement in local parish organizations than first-generation males may be willing to grant them.[14] No matter how hard its members try, no culture can remain static. To fail to change is to court death.

Understanding Cognitive Cultures

With so much on the line, therefore, parishes shared between two or more cultural groups must transition at some point from Stage 4, where two parallel communities exist side by side, to Stages 5 and 6, where true inter-cultural adaptation and integration will take place. This requires becoming aware of, and to a certain extent comfortable in, the cognitive culture of each of the parish's component groups. One sociologist has listed several dimensions, or continuums, along which the basic cognitive grounding of a culture may vary. These should not be read as two opposite poles; most cultures exist somewhere in between, but closer to one end than the other.[15]

- *Collectivism vs. Individualism:* In international surveys, the United States routinely registers as one of the most individualistic cultures in the world. In individualistic cultures, the individual's needs have priority over those of the group.[16] In collectivist cultures, on the other hand, the individual is defined by his/her place in the larger group, and the group's needs for honor, prosperity, and internal harmony take precedence over any needs or desires an individual may have. Loyalty and obedience to the group is the highest value.

- *Hierarchy vs. Equality:* Americans also assume that all persons are, or should be, equal. Authority or status is earned, not granted automatically. If an American meets the mayor, the governor, or even the president, he or she feels free to tell that official what he or she thinks about an issue. In real life, of course, America is a lot less equal a country than we think we are, and communication "up the hierarchy" is never as direct as it is made out to be. But we still assume equality. In hierarchical cultures, on the other hand, authority and status are attached automatically to one's position in the group. It would be disrespectful for lower persons to contradict a higher person, so communication is more indirect or carried out by mediators. While Americans take silence to mean consent, in hierarchical cultures it often means that the person we are talking to disagrees with us but is unwilling to say so out loud.

- *Low vs. High Tolerance for Ambiguity:* In cultures with a low tolerance for ambiguity, there are explicit rules for behavior that everyone is expected to follow. Cultures with a high tolerance for ambiguity allow their members more freedom.

- *Gender Roles:* An outgrowth of the two previous dimensions of cognitive culture is the roles assigned to men and women. Cultures with a low tolerance for ambiguity will demand strict adherence to gender roles; cultures with a higher tolerance will allow men and women more freedom to follow lifestyles more usually taken by the other gender—"Mr. Mom," for example, or women soldiers. Hierarchical cultures will also rank one gender over the other; more egalitarian cultures (at least in theory) will not.

- *The Meaning of Time:* Some cultures have a "lived experience of time"—time is subordinated to the needs of the group to maintain and foster its internal harmony. Time may be thought of as cyclic, repeating past patterns. People in the United States, in contrast, see time as abstract and a value in itself ("Time is money"). Meetings start on time, and it is important to use time efficiently. Time is thought of as linear, progressing toward a future that must be anticipated and, if possible, shaped.

People reading the above list probably find themselves instinctively agreeing with one side and wondering how anyone could possibly hold the opposite view. The important thing to realize is that the point of view that you or I find difficult even to fathom is as instinctive and natural to members of another culture as our instinctive assumptions are to us.

These instinctive cognitive assumptions and values will manifest themselves in behaviors that can cause annoyance and misunderstandings among parishioners from other cultural groups, if they do not understand their cultural basis. Persons from more hierarchical cultures may be less willing to make eye contact in interactions. They may agree with the leader at a meeting, not because they really intend to follow a given plan of action, but because it would be disrespectful for them to disagree. They may not start a meeting until everyone has shown up (and, with nonlinear concepts of time, this may not happen until quite a bit after the scheduled hour), and not until everyone has had a chance to greet each other and get caught up with each other's lives. Leaders may be chosen because of their rank or status in the group, even if someone else is more technically competent. Clergy from hierarchical cultures may expect automatic deference and submission that Anglo Americans may be unwilling to grant.

It is also important to realize that cultures are not static; they do change, especially when their members come into contact with each other. Thus, recent studies have found that Hispanics who have lived a long time in the United States, or who were born here, have become less socially conservative than those who have recently arrived—although they are still more likely than Anglo Americans to ascribe to traditional gender roles and to disapprove of sex outside of marriage or unmarried pregnancy.[17]

Challenges to US Catholic Parishes

While most of the immigrants from Latin America are Catholic, reflecting the solidly Catholic cultures of their respective homelands, a significant percentage of them do not remain in the church after arriving here. Nearly one in four Hispanic adults in the United States are former Catholics. These are overall figures; the percentage of Catholics is even lower among some nationality groups such as Guatemalan immigrants or Puerto Ricans. The rate of leaving Catholicism increases the longer Hispanics are in this country: one poll found that, while 61 percent of Hispanics born outside the United States identify as Catholics, only half of those born in the United States with parents who were also born here, say they are Catholics. Of those who leave the church, half join conservative Protestant, evangelical, or Pentecostal churches; a quarter join mainline Protestant churches; and another quarter drop out of religion altogether.[18] Hispanic young adults are the least likely to remain Catholic and the most likely to claim that they have no religion at all.[19] Hispanics who remain Catholic are significantly less likely to say they are very religious (43 percent), as compared to those who are Protestant (60 percent).[20] A quote from a recent Gallup Poll Report sums up these findings:

> A majority of Hispanics in America continue to identify as Catholic, although the Catholic percentage among Hispanics appears to be decreasing and the youngest Hispanics in America today are less likely to be Catholic than those who are older. Additionally, those Hispanics who are Catholic are much less religious than those who are Protestant.[21]

In recent decades, the total number of Catholics in the United States has risen from 45.6 million in 1965 to 67 million today, while the percentage of Americans who are Catholic has stayed relatively constant at around 25 percent. This compares favorably with Mainline Protestant denominations that have decreased in both total number and in percentage of the population. But the numerical strength of US Catholics is due in large part to the large number of new Catholic immigrants from Latin America and other parts of the world. Their average age is 27. "Hispanic ministry in parishes is essentially ministry with youth and young families, an opportunity to shape a new generation of Catholics."[22] Yet only 26 percent of parishes have a pastoral leader dedicated primarily to working with Hispanic youth and young adults. Only four in ten parishes with Hispanic ministry have any programs targeting Hispanic youth.[23] If our parishes do not make them welcome, they will not remain Catholic long.

Why They Leave

Studies of former Catholics among Hispanic immigrants have found that a primary attraction of Evangelical and Pentecostal churches is the greater sense of community that these churches offer. Catholic parishes in the United States are larger than the parishes to which the immigrants had been accustomed in their home countries and, with the merging of parishes due to the clergy shortage, they are becoming larger still. Hispanics complain of the "coldness" of the Anglos who attend Catholic Sunday Mass in these huge parishes: they don't know each other (and they certainly don't know the lone Hispanic who happens to wander in), and they don't linger to talk and get acquainted after the liturgy is over. "They rush right out to the parking lot, to see who can get out first." In contrast, the average Protestant evangelical congregation contains two hundred members, all of whom know each other. Everyone is Hispanic; often from the same country or even from the same village or region. The pastor is also Hispanic and familiar with the culture.[24]

A main characteristic of the religion of the immigrants' home countries was that it was of and for the people. "The mainstreaming of United States Catholicism, its strong middle-class orientation and the increasing professionalization of its ministers both clerical and lay, are the source of considerable discomfort for Hispanics."[25] The more educated Anglo Catholics might even look down on the newcomers' popular religious practices as "pre-Vatican II" and unenlightened. In contrast, the Protestant churches "are perceived as churches of the poor and for the poor . . . Generally, their buildings are much simpler and often these are 'storefront' churches."[26] The worship that goes on inside is done in the style the worshippers themselves choose, rather than being dictated by an upper-middle-class clergy. Because they are "of the poor and for the poor," the members of Evangelical and Pentecostal congregations are more willing to become actively involved in helping each other to deal with the many problems that afflict the poor: "addictions, violence, and strained relationships between family members. The Catholic Church, on the other hand, is seen as being uncomfortable with poverty and as not dealing with the real problems that poor people generally experience."[27] To quote one former Catholic Mexican woman, now a member of a Pentecostal church in downtown Los Angeles, "There are so many gangs around here. And [my church] is really doing something to stop the violence."[28]

Most immigrants, Hispanic and otherwise, have come to the United States from environments where religion and spirituality permeated all aspects of their existence. In the old country, this kind of religion was passed down by mothers and grandmothers to the children—notice the role of her mother in Ana Maria Diaz-Stevens's description of her Puerto Rican childhood, quoted in chapter 1 (above, p. 20). The immigrants are often cut off from this chain of memory when they come to the United States as teens or young adults, and when they establish their own families, they are unable to replicate the instinctive and pervasive religion of their childhood: "a faith that is characterized by an explicit affirmation of God's transcendence, strong convictions about God's will in certain matters of morality founded on biblical teaching, a confidence in God's power to work miracles and especially to heal."[29] The small, all-Hispanic, Evangelical congregations seem to offer this kind of religious atmosphere in a way that the religiously alien, Anglo Catholic parishes do not.

Another attraction of the Protestant churches is the opportunity they offer for religious leadership. Many migrants are barred from ordained, or even lay, parish leadership positions by their lower educational levels, or by the fact that they are married.

> In contrast to Catholicism, Alcance Victoria allows married men without education to have active and rewarding careers in ministry. In the congregation, men discover their entrepreneurial potential. Through ministerial work in the congregation, they can improve their lot in life and live comfortably. The congregation expects their ministers to live well, because ministers symbolize the aspirations of the group. A man can come to church, marry the woman he has dreamed about, become active in ministry, and move up through the Alcance Victoria/Victory Outreach chain of command.[30]

The church encourages these men to become pastors of their own churches: "This is the path taken by hundreds of men in Victory Outreach/Alcance Victoria."[31] In some churches, the women, too, have opportunities to exercise religious leadership. In others, the opportunity to obtain a husband who is religiously active and ambitious for higher church positions, instead of a man who drinks, gambles, and is physically abusive to her, is itself an attraction.

A study of the storefront Pentecostal church in the preceding paragraph sums up these attractions:

> Most of the "lapsed Catholics" came to Alcance Victoria because they enjoyed the company of others, the feeling of belonging, the music, the message of security and control over life . . . In the congregation they find emotional security, friendship, and intimacy. For immigrants and Mexican Americans who lack social skills, the congregation functions as a mechanism of cultural brokerage. Symbolically and physically secluded from so many other centers in Los Angeles, they find in Alcance Victoria vibrant fellowship where they remake self, community, and the nation.[32]

Or, to put it in the words of Alcance Victoria's pastor, "Alcance Victoria is successful because we are meeting the needs of the people."[33]

What Can a Parish Do?

The new immigrant ethnic groups thus pose a challenge to the American Church—a challenge to renew ourselves, to become better Christians. When new arrivals say they are looking for "interesting and relevant worship services, for committed and understanding priests, and for a laity that shows equal concern for worship, spiritual growth, and concern for others,"[34] they are calling us to growth beyond our comfort zones, beyond our own narrow cultural articulation of what it means to be Catholic. A basic premise of this book is that, by learning to view our Catholic faith through more than one set of cultural lenses, we will enrich the Catholicity (i.e., the universality) of our parishes. To do so, however, we need an awareness of cognitive culture—the deep, unspoken assumptions that shape our way of thinking. We need to understand how the values of our and others' cultures underlie the way we behave. We need to create times and spaces in which we can share how each culture, as Pope Francis said, enriches Catholicism. If we can do this, then both we and our parishes will better image the God who is so much more than we can imagine.

Growth hurts. Stepping out of our culture is difficult. Trying to join two or more cultural groups into a single worshipping community will necessarily involve conflicts, hurt feelings, and in some cases, even angry departures. How can a parish assist all of its members—both the long-standing ones and the new arrivals—to understand, learn from, and change each other so as to truly become the *one, holy, universal, and apostolic* church we are called to be? This section of the chapter will list some ways to gently encourage intercultural understanding, and to deal with difficulties along the way.

Welcoming Practices

The most important roadblock cited by arrivals from new ethnic groups was that they did not feel welcome in Catholic parishes. It may be true that parishes are sincerely trying to welcome members from different cultures, but what matters is that they often are not *perceived* as doing so. What are some of the things parishes might do to make their welcome more evident?

- Given the importance of *convivencia* (the time before or after Mass when parishioners get together and catch up on each other's lives) to many ethnic groups,[35] setting aside a time for this essential function is important. Many parishes often have "coffee and donut" hours after Mass—these should be expanded, and members of all cultural groups in the parish should be consulted on how to attract more persons to them.

- It is hard to stand on the edge of a parish social affair—a picnic, a Lenten fish fry, even the coffee and donut hour—and not recognize anyone. How to break into such a group, especially if your English is not all that good? A parish could deputize a dozen or more extroverted persons, from the various ethnic and generational cultures it wants to attract to these functions, to watch for new arrivals standing hesitantly at the door, to approach them, introduce themselves, and take the newcomers under their wing until they feel at home.

- It is vital that each group be able to worship in its own language—not merely in its verbal language of English, Spanish, Tagalog, or whatever, but also in the language of its symbols, music, gestures, and ceremonies. And not only worship at Mass, but also in retreats, novenas, ceremonies for *quinceaneras*, and special festivals to celebrate each ethnic group's patron saints. Sponsoring traditional religious observations and offering Mass in its own language are powerful symbols that the ethnic group is an accepted and valued part of the parish.[36] Certain special celebrations (e.g., Holy Thursday or the Easter Vigil) might be offered for all ethnicities together and include all the various languages of the parish as a sign of parish unity. Ecclesial movements such as the Cursillo Movement or the Charismatic Renewal may also serve to unite participants across ethnic lines. Eventually and gradually over time, the number and importance of these bilingual or trilingual celebrations may increase.

After all, the second generation of the new immigrant group may no longer be attracted to a worship style so thoroughly redolent of the old country, and their religious needs, too, must be met.

- Most American parishes are quite large and getting larger. We might take a lesson from Protestant megachurches that assume their members do not know each other and deliberately plan weekly activities to draw new and existing members into contact with each other. Some of these might be

  - Small faith communities: These could be lay-led (a good way to surface leadership among the members of new ethnic groups) and could be composed of like or unlike members along any of several dimensions—age, ethnicity, gender, etc.

  - "Adopt a family": One Protestant megachurch assigns all new members to a "shepherd" who contacts them as soon as possible, helps them get involved and find friends in whatever church activities they express an interest, and finds out about any joys the larger church can help celebrate with them or any griefs the church can help them to bear.[37] Similarly, parishes might ask long-standing members each to take an immigrant family under their wing and help them with difficulties such as children who need tutoring in English or math, parents who need help learning English, figuring out a government form, or using a computer, and so on. And the immigrant family, in return, might help the children in the English-speaking family learn a foreign language!

  - Sharing life stories: Parish youth might be deputized to conduct oral histories, both of the long-standing members whose memories go back to the parish's earliest days, and also of the older immigrants who can share what life was like in the old country. Both of these groups are the last living representatives in this country of what it was like to grow up surrounded by a pervasive Catholic culture that the young have not experienced. Another possibility is to gather members of both ethnic groups by age and have them share common experiences of navigating high school and dating, or of marrying and raising small children, or of experiencing old age.

- The Bishops' Committee on Cultural Diversity stated that the highest degree of welcoming was when all component groups of the parish became so thoroughly united that they shared equally in parish decision-making.

The committee recommended the implementation of cross-cultural programs where parishioners could develop both spiritually and as leaders.[38] Some immigrant groups (e.g., Guatemalans) have a strong tradition of lay spiritual leadership. This could be fostered and shared.

Evangelizing

In addition to the various ways in which parishes may make all their members feel welcomed, it is also important for parishes to invite nonmembers to join them. As one former Catholic explained, "I joined [my Pentecostal church] because they asked me to come." This does not necessarily mean going from door to door or accosting shoppers in parking lots. What it *does* mean, first of all, is to move beyond the denial stage to find out just how many persons of a targeted ethnic group there actually are in the area, where they live and work, and what their needs are. Networking is also important: potential members will be more likely to join us if invited by someone they already know. On the other side, the reluctance of parishioners to invite must also be addressed. It helps to have actual events to invite someone to, preferably planned by parishioners from the targeted group who know what would appeal to them. Current parishioners will find it easier to invite their neighbors and coworkers to something specific and attractive.

Evangelization also involves catechesis—both of youth and adults—tailored to their language and culture. A single faith formation program for both immigrant and Anglo-American youth, or a single RCIA program for all the adults in the parish, will not be enough. One recent study of shared parishes noted that immigrants' faith formation needed to include dealing with their cultural disorientation, insecurity, and separation from their extended families:

> The English catechetical program, on the other hand, addressed a different cultural milieu, one that included low birthrates, the outmigration of young people of marriage age, and, most important, multiple activities available for school-age children. It was a smaller program than the Spanish one, and a desire to compete for families' limited time translated to easier requirements. Conversely, the Spanish program depended on a commitment to sacraments as cultural rites of passages and tackled religious literacy through comprehensive educational discipline.[39]

It may even be necessary to have *three* catechetical programs: one for native Anglo youth, one for first-generation immigrants (in their native language), and one for the second generation of ethnic youth (in English) that specifically addresses their uneasy tension of living between the traditional culture of their parents and the attractions of secular American culture. But this, too, could present problems if the older children in a family attended one catechetical program and the younger ones the other—which child's required parental meetings should the parents attend?

In designing such programs, it is important to have the input of the ethnic group whose family members and friends will be involved. One author notes that the most vital evangelization movement in 1940s and 1950s Puerto Rico "came from ordinary rural laymen, who were organized into a missionary institute called *Hermanos Cheos* to combat the Protestantization of the countryside."[40] Focus groups of parish members (conducted in their language) could be held to learn what their main evangelization concerns are and to surface suggestions for how to address them.

Service Provision

New immigrants whom we invite to our parishes need more than catechesis in the faith. They may also need classes in English as a second language, in health education, in job skills (especially computers), or in basic literacy and GED preparation. They may need child care, immigration and legal assistance, translation help, and help in finding employment or housing. A recent study[41] of Latino congregations, Catholic and Protestant, in the Chicago area found that the Catholic parishes provided more services[42] than the Protestant churches, whether Mainline, Evangelical, or Pentecostal. But Catholic Hispanics were less likely to *use* these services: 60 percent of the study's Catholic respondents reported receiving no help at all from the church, as compared to less than half of Mainline and Evangelical Protestants and only 30 percent of Pentecostals. The researcher speculated that this might be because the Catholic parishes were larger (and could offer more programs) but that their services were more formalized, while the Protestants' services were more individualized and personal. The researcher also noted that the Pentecostal and Evangelical churches were more likely to have Latino lay leadership, who may be more aware of their congregants' needs and more approachable by those seeking help.

While lay leadership by persons of the same ethnicity may be helpful in making a parish's services known to immigrants in need, services offered cross-culturally can provide opportunities for each group within a shared parish to enrich their knowledge of each other. The Bishops' "Best Practices" booklet describes one shared parish in which

[a]ny need of services for one group is communicated to the other groups. For example, during Thanksgiving and Christmas holidays, families from each of the language groups that are in need are sponsored by another family or parish organization that does not necessarily come from the same language group.[43]

In meeting the needs of ethnic groups new to the parish, it is especially important not to neglect the mundane daily needs of youth and families. Establishing and fostering youth groups are one of the most important pastoral initiatives a parish can undertake and should precede all else. Depending on the pastoral needs of each parish, there may be one youth group for each ethnicity, or a single common group that helps all the youth of the parish get to know each other. Trips and activities were key attractors mentioned by Hispanic respondents, but simply providing a safe space to hang out and share the problems of growing up are also important. Hispanic respondents also suggest having "Family Nights" in which parishioners and invited potential parishioners for all ages can share a meal, view a movie, or engage in other fun activities. Yet one study foresaw a looming crisis "as thousands of culturally competent pastoral leaders approach the age of retirement," and few younger Catholics are available to replace them in offering such programs.[44]

Difficulties

Of course, none of this is easy. Any parish initiative will inevitably bring conflicts:

- *Conflicts over worship styles.* Deep and subconscious differences in the grounding cognitive and value aspects of their respective cultures will lead parishioners from different ethnic groups to resonate to quite different styles of liturgical worship. It will be detrimental to the spiritual life and worship of a group's members if the music, the length of the service, or the presence and behavior of children go against their instinctive assumptions and values. Changes (on both sides) will need to be introduced gradually, and it may take an entire generation before the worship styles become truly united. Until then, separate worship services in each language will continue to be important.

- *Use of parish facilities:* As the Bishops' "Best Practices" booklet observed, newcomers from different ethnic groups, if they are truly welcomed, "develop a sense of belonging to the parish that enables them to expect

more resources on the way, such as a better schedule for their Sunday
Liturgy, the use of the new hall, a catechetical program that allows
parents to teach the faith to their own children, the celebration of traditions particular to their culture, and so forth." Meanwhile, longtime
parishioners may come to resent the newcomers and think they are
"taking over" the parish.[45] In addition, differences in cognitive culture
regarding how each group views and values time may lead one group to
become upset if the other does not plan ahead and reserve the facilities,
or stays in a room longer than they had signed up for.

• *Extern clergy:* If a pastor who speaks the language of the newcomers
is not available in the diocese, priests may be imported from a country
where that language is spoken. This has not always been successful.
Studies of extern clergy in the New York Archdiocese found they usually came from Spain or Latin America for personal reasons (such as
to complete their education in an American degree program), and had
a reputation for shallow commitment to their largely Puerto Rican
parishes.[46] Korean priests, one critic charged, came on four-year terms
and were not invested in the future reality of the US Korean immigrants—especially of the second-generation Korean-Americans who
were less able even to speak the same language.[47] The "Best Practices"
booklet noted that there is a danger of the extern priest becoming the "de
facto pastor" of the ethnic group, usurping the authority of the pastor.[48]
Conversely, appointing an extern priest as pastor may alienate the Anglo
parishioners, especially if he expects the deference from them that he
had been accustomed to in his former country. Finally, dioceses have
often not been sensitive to national and class differences between the
ethnic priest assigned to a parish and the ethnic parishioners to whom
he is expected to minister. Assigning a Spanish Basque priest to a Puerto
Rican parish, or a Nigerian priest to an African-American parish, and
expecting that everyone will get along fine may be naïve. One early critic
even argued that knowledge of parishioners' culture was more important
than being able to speak their language.[49]

Finally, all this attention to the newly-arrived ethnic group may cause the
long-standing members of the parish to feel that their own contributions
have been dismissed. Especially in the older areas of many US cities, there
are remnants of parishioners, now in their 60s and 70s, who have supported
"their" church with their time, talent, and treasure for half a century or
more. The parish is the setting of their fondest life memories: they were

married there; their children were baptized and attended school there; they may even have been baptized and schooled there as children themselves. They have decades-long friendships with other parishioners, and equally long-accustomed ways of doing things. Now an entire cherished way of life and a tight-knit community is threatened.

All of these difficulties are serious and must be dealt with. In the past, Catholics have been uncomfortable with intra-parish conflicts, and have tended to avoid dealing with them. This avoidance tendency is strengthened by the cognitive and value cultures of both long-standing and newly-arrived parishioners, but is often expressed in different, and less than constructive, ways. The individualistic bias to American culture often blinds long-standing parishioners to the ways in which larger parish and diocesan structures disempower new ethnic groups.[50] And a common American tactic for avoiding conflict is something critics have called "moral minimalism"—instead of working through a problem in person, they call in "the authorities" to handle it.[51] In a parish, this might involve a teacher in the parish school complaining to the principal about how "they" were leaving the classroom out of order after Sunday religion class, rather than working out the difficulty with the religious education teacher involved. Meanwhile, persons from collectivist cultures are also likely to avoid conflict in order to save group "face."[52]

Another source of conflict is often the deep pain arising from the real losses all the parishioners have experienced in sharing the parish. These losses need to be acknowledged and grieved. Long-standing parishioners need the time, understanding, and space to express their sense of loss of their own space. "Words like *my grandparents built this parish*, or *it was so difficult for us to finally have a parish we can call our own and now they may take over,* express feelings of uncertainty, loss, and even mourning that are quite real and need to be taken seriously."[53] Equally important is the pain experienced by newcomers to a strange land and a strange church. "Most immigrants were forced to leave their home and families because of poverty, violence, or persecution and live in a different country with a different language and culture."[54] They, too, feel loss. The booklets published by the Bishops' Committee on Cultural Diversity in the Church contain suggestions for parishes dealing with this sense of loss.

It is, of course, hard to do any of the things suggested in this chapter, and we will never do them perfectly. But even to begin, however tentatively and imperfectly, could yield wonderful results. As one priest put it:

> The point . . . is that the question of the liberation of others is the question of the liberation of me. Can I, in my relationship with others, allow them to challenge me—to come in touch with me? Can I really come to understand that I'm incomplete—that there's a vast degree of riches within me that I haven't even begun to be in touch with? And that there's a vast degree of poverty and garbage within me that I don't even begin to be conscious of?[55]

This is what we are called to do for each other when we relate across cultures in love. And ethnic cultures are not the only ones we need to cross. The next section of this book will look at *generational* cultures and how different age groups in our parishes see Catholicism through generational eyes.

4

Generational Cultures
An Overview

"Generation after generation will offer joyful worship in you."
—Tobit 13:11

Not only do our parishes need to speak the Good News to various ethnic cultures, we also need to address different generational cultures. Just as we are all shaped by the childhood experiences peculiar to our social class and ethnic group, we are also influenced by the particular material culture and societal events that characterized the decade in which we were raised. Children are like little sponges: just by observing the adults around them, they pick up an optimistic or a pessimistic view of the future, priorities about what things are important or unimportant, and basic assumptions about how the world works. Scholars call these mindsets "collective mentalities": they are the "broad, deep mental structures—world views, basic values, mind sets and characteristic ways of thinking" common to persons who have experienced the same set of formative influences.[1] In the terminology of this book, we would say that the children are absorbing the cognitive and value aspects of their culture. So if we compare a child who spent his/her free time outside and unsupervised—riding bicycles down relatively un-trafficked streets, playing hopscotch or stickball—with one born later who was always being chauffeured by parents to "play dates" and formally-organized sports leagues, we would find that they grew up in cultures that were in some ways every bit as different as if one had been born in England and the other in France. Children whose parents lost jobs and homes due to a pervasive economic downturn, or who practiced regular "atom bomb drills" at school and listened to war reports on the TV news, developed cognitive cultural outlooks that were profoundly different from those of children growing up in times of peace and prosperity—outlooks that would remain different for the rest of their lives. In the most basic aspects of our cognitive culture, we are all products of the era in which we grew up.

We don't question this worldview while we are children; it is simply the basic background from which we think and act. It is only in late adolescence that we become intellectually able, for the first time, to form our own opinions on the cognitive and value aspects of the culture we have inherited from our childhood. We accept whatever in it seems true and consistent with the reality we see, and we reject what seems wrong or inconsistent to us. We have at that moment our first and only "fresh encounter" with the larger world *that will become the lens through which we will view it for the rest of our lives.* As one political scientist stated, "late adolescence and early adulthood are the formative years during which a distinctive personal outlook on politics emerges."[2] A similar claim could be made for our outlooks on just about anything else—including God and religion. The adult opinions and mindset we form around age twenty become our "native" generational culture that colors forever the way we think about the "foreign" generational cultures that preceded and will follow us. The farther removed these generations are from us in time, the more difficult it is for us truly to understand their mental and emotional worldview—and for them to understand us. As one psychologist recently wrote: "Asking young people today to adopt the personality and attitudes of a previous time is like asking an adult American to instantly become Chinese."[3]

Why is it so hard to change our initial adult worldview? First, psychologists have found that we all engage in "motivated reasoning"—our previous opinions and emotions influence how we approach new facts. We disproportionately pay attention to information that supports our point of view and resist information that disconfirms it. This is even easier to do today than in previous decades because "the way we now consume information— through the Facebook links of friends, or tweets that lack nuance or context, or 'narrowcast' and often highly ideological media that have relatively small, like-minded audiences"—makes it less likely that we will ever even *hear* viewpoints that are different from our own.[4]

In addition to motivated reasoning, most people also have a "social desirability bias"—we find disagreeing with our friends unpleasant, and so we tend to adopt the same opinions they have. As part of our bonding with them, we tell and retell among ourselves the stories, jokes, and metaphors that reinforce the reasons why *our way* is the correct and logical way to think and act. Thus, as the years pass, the cognitive and value culture we adopted when we were young adults thus becomes less and less amenable to change, no matter how far its assumptions gradually depart from the actual situations of our changing society. We are usually blind to these growing discrepancies; it is our own young adult children who have the "fresh eyes" to see them.

As an example of how this works out in real life, we might consider someone who was born in the 1920s and grew up during the Great Depression. Such a person would absorb, in his or her childhood, the basic assumptions that money is tight, that leftovers should never be wasted, and that family and community are precious resources to help them weather hard times. Then suppose that this person came of age during World War II: he or she would learn to sacrifice even more for a noble cause. These formative experiences would shape that generation's life ever afterward: they would save money and avoid going into debt, reuse plastic bags, give their kids the toys they themselves had never had, respect government and authority, support keeping America militarily strong, and so forth.

But what growing-up experiences will their 1950s era children have? They will be fortunate enough to experience material security—but have to hide under their desks during nuclear bomb drills. Their parents will expect them to respect authority—while they consult Dr. Benjamin Spock's child-care book on how to foster their children's independence and initiative. When these children turn eighteen in the 1960s, they will have questions that target the inconsistencies in their upbringing—inconsistencies between what their parents said and how they acted, as well as inconsistencies between what they learned at home or at school and how changes in the larger society were rendering these lessons outdated. All upbringings have such inconsistencies. And so they will begin to question some of the cognitive and value aspects of their parents' culture, which are that culture's deepest and most foundational parts and therefore precisely the ones it is the most threatening to question.

When shifts in generational cultures happen, the previous generation is often aghast. The young seem to be cavalierly discarding the very values and practices that their elders had worked so hard to defend. Even more confusingly, the young often "mix and match" beliefs that their elders had assigned to opposite ideological camps, accepting some and refusing others. Conservative political beliefs in the 1920s and 1930s, for example, had "packaged" isolationism in foreign policy with a suspicion of domestic welfare programs such as Social Security—despite the lack of any logical connection between the two.[5] "Neoconservatives" of the 1980s and 1990s, in contrast, remained suspicious of domestic welfare programs but changed their foreign policy beliefs to support active military intervention abroad. Older generations usually become so accustomed to viewing the world through one set of assumptions and to linking together one "package" of views on disparate issues that they find it impossible to understand why the younger generation does not see things in the same way.

Of course, not all people born in a given year will automatically adopt a single common worldview when they reach young adulthood. Our generational cohort is only one of several "social locations" that influence us: our race or ethnicity, our social class, and even our gender also determine the beliefs, opinions, and values we develop. Studies have shown that a given situation or event affects young adults in different ways, depending on the young adult's position in these other social locations. The Civil Rights Movement, for example, has been cited as a key influence by African Americans who were young adults in the 1960s, but not by White Americans the same age—nor, for that matter, by African Americans born after 1970. Women who were young adults in the early 1970s are more likely than men their age to say that the Women's Movement was a key influence on them.[6] Thus, it is not inconceivable that a single generation could contain antagonistic "generation units": whites and blacks the same age, men and women the same age, or upper-class and working-class young adults, with diametrically opposed worldviews.

Other, more psychological, influences exist as well. Every generation also contains a "cognitive minority": individuals who, for whatever reason, refuse to accept the worldviews and values of the majority of their peers. For example, both George W. Bush and Mitt Romney were young adults in the late 1960s. Yet, unlike the majority of their middle-class, white peers, they adopted conservative and establishment-oriented worldviews. Cognitive minorities are often the vanguard of a future generation, reflecting attitudes and worldviews that will become common in another ten or twenty years. The problem is, however, that one aspect of the worldview that cognitive minorities adopt in their young adulthood *is precisely their embattled minority status.* Thus, many political and religious conservatives, who currently exercise strong influence among America's governmental, business, and cultural elites, still continue to see themselves as much weaker and more precarious than their liberal opponents—even when that self-image no longer corresponds to reality.[7] Liberals, meanwhile, have today become a minority within many sectors of society—absorbing a self-image of powerlessness that, in turn, may persist in the future beyond its objective reality.

Each generational cohort thus clings to the cognitive assumptions and cultural values of its own young adulthood and raises the next generation accordingly. That generation, in its own young adulthood, discards the beliefs and values of its elders that appear outdated or inconsistent. And the elders, in turn, react with the same horror and condemnation with which *their* parents had once reacted to them. Thus, there is often a cultural oscillation: between liberal and conservative eras in politics, between romantic and realist fashions in literature, between hedonistic and more straitlaced sensibilities in morality, between activism and apathy in social movements.[8]

There is, admittedly, a certain amount of fuzziness in the sociological concept of a generation that some critics have noted. Generations may vary in length: in times of rapid societal change, even five or ten years' difference in age may lead to sharply divergent worldviews, while in more placid times a single sociological generation may span several biological generations. There are also no hard and fast boundaries between one generation and the next, and persons born on the "cusp" between two labeled generations may exhibit characteristics of both. As one author notes, generational cohorts may be "clearest at their centers, but blurred and fuzzy at the edges."[9] One generation's members may not even be conscious of themselves as a generation, or they may actively resist being lumped together in this way because they see themselves as individuals. It is also important to distinguish the impact of generational culture (growing up in a particular time) from life-cycle effects (having changing interests as one gets older) and period effects (Pearl Harbor, the Kennedy assassination, and 9/11 affected everybody alive at the time).[10] If Americans in their seventies are more conservative, more religious, or more pessimistic than Americans in their twenties, is this because they were children in a more conservative, religious, or pessimistic time (generational culture), or because all persons naturally develop these traits as they get older (life-cycle effects)? Or did some specific event happen that affected *all* Americans, of whatever age, who lived through it (period effects)?

Given this conceptual fuzziness, many sociologists have tended to resist using the concept. Sociologists studying religion, however, have begun to make extensive use of it, since both North Americans and Europeans often show pronounced generational differences in their religious beliefs and practices. It has become crucially important for churches to know whether the young adults who do not express an interest in joining them today will return to the fold once they marry and settle down, or whether they will retain their current disinterest. Congregations are also wrestling with generational change within the ethnic groups who attend their services: how can they appeal to first-generation immigrants from the old country who have one configuration of cultural values and assumptions, and also to the immigrants' children and grandchildren who grew up in a very different environment?

In order to answer questions such as these, it is important to know how different generational cohorts tend to view the world, and also the specific role of religion and church within this worldview. The next section of this chapter will outline some of the categories the popular media have used to label the generational cohorts among Americans and will report on some of the sociological and psychological findings about their overall characteristics. The following chapter will focus specifically on the *religious* characteristics of these generations, as they are manifested among American Catholics. At the present, we are only considering generations of white, middle-class Americans because that is whom sociologists have predominantly studied so far. Later, however, we will also consider generational differences among Hispanics, Asians, Africans, and African-Americans.

A Brief Description of Generations in the United States

While some authors divide things differently or use different terminology, most writers label the generational cohorts among white, middle-class Americans as indicated in Table 1.

Generational Cohorts in the United States: Formative Influences

The "Greatest Generation"—Born 1915–1929

Childhood Environment:

- Transportation—the popularization of the automobile
- Media—early radio, films
- For urban dwellers—solidly ethnic neighborhoods
- Economic prosperity for older members; the Great Depression for younger members

Adolescence and Early Adulthood:

- The Great Depression
- World War II

The "Silent Generation"—Born 1930–1945

Childhood Environment:

- World War II
- Media—radio, films
- For Urban dwellers—solidly ethnic neighborhoods
- The Great Depression for older members

- Demographically—smaller than the preceding or subsequent generations

Adolescence and Early Adulthood:

- The Korean War
- Economic prosperity
- The Cold War

The "Baby Boomers"—Born 1946–1961

Childhood Environment:

- The Cold War
- Economic prosperity
- Suburbanization
- The Civil Rights Movement
- Media—television, transistor radios, rock and roll
- Demographically—larger than the preceding or subsequent generations

Adolescence and Early Adulthood:

- Vietnam, Watergate
- Environmental issues

Generation X—Born 1962–1981

Childhood Environment:

- Vietnam and Watergate for the older members
- Suburbanization
- Divorced parents
- Environmental issues—gas shortages
- The Challenger Explosion
- The Iran Hostage crisis
- Economic "stagflation"
- Demographically—smaller than the preceding or subsequent generations

Adolescence and Early Adulthood:

- 1980s' recession
- Media—personal computers/internet

Millennials—Born 1982–1999

Childhood Environment:
- Economic prosperity in the 1990s
- Columbine and other high school shootings
- "Helicopter parents"
- Demographically—larger than the preceding or subsequent generations
- Media—personal computers/internet

Adolescence and Early Adulthood:
- 9/11 and the War on Terror
- The Great Recession
- The Obama elections
- College debt

Post-Millennials—Born 2000 and after

Childhood Environment:
- 9/11 and the War on Terror, Iraq, and Afghanistan
- The Great Recession
- Media—smart phones, Facebook, Twitter, instant messaging, etc.
- Demographically—relative large birth rate 2000–2006; sharp drop thereafter

The Greatest Generation: Americans born between 1915 and 1929 were shaped by the hardships of the Great Depression in their childhood and adolescence. They learned early on to sacrifice their own plans for the greater good of their families and society. They had strong experiences of community connectedness: most grew up either in rural areas and small towns, or in the tight-knit ethnic neighborhoods of America's large cities. As they came of age, the United States entered World War II, in which many of them fought. They postponed marriage until after the war, and many followed the American Dream by being the first in their families to buy their own home and raise their families in the newly built suburbs. Because of their childhoods during the Roosevelt administration, this generation tended to vote Democratic in subsequent elections.

The Silent Generation: The defining characteristic of this generation is that its members were too young to fight in World War II. The Korean War, in which some of them did serve, was a much more ambiguous conflict. Social commentators therefore tended to compare this generation's members unfavorably with the heroic previous generation. Critics accused them of passivity and lack of civic commitment. The label "Silent Generation" was coined by *Time* magazine in 1951 to describe them, and it was *not* a compliment. They have tended to be more Republican in their voting patterns than the Greatest Generation. Today, they are disproportionately represented among the audiences for conservative radio and television talk shows, are more likely to express anger and frustration with government, and are the most pessimistic about the country's future. One observer noted that they are also over-represented at Tea Party rallies.[11] They are the "whitest" and the smallest of the current generations, and their generation is the only one in American history not to have had a member elected president. And yet this negative image may not be totally justified: it was also the Silent Generation that began the modern Civil Rights and student protest movements. Like the Greatest Generation, most members of this generation also grew up in tightly-knit communities, whether in small rural towns or in homogeneous urban ethnic neighborhoods, and moved to suburbs as adults.

The Baby Boomers: The oldest members of this generational cohort were born nine months after the end of World War II, and birth rates did not fall to pre-1946 levels again until 1961. The sheer size of the Boomer generation shaped all of its experiences, to the detriment of the much smaller generations before and after them. Unlike previous generations, the Baby Boomers were less likely to grow up in small, homogeneous communities, being more familiar with larger-scale, suburban lifestyles. They were the first TV and transistor radio generation, and the first to be targeted by mass marketers selling them hula hoops, Davy Crockett caps, and 45 rpm rock and roll records. Their consumerist upbringing influenced their attitudes toward finances and saving for the rest of their lives. Many members of this generation have not saved enough for their looming retirement: a full two-thirds expect to remain in the labor force longer as a result. While initially more liberal in their voting patterns than the Silent Generation, 53 percent now say that their political views became more conservative as they grew older—a life-cycle rather than a generational effect.

Some commentators, as well as the US Census Bureau, divide the Baby Boom Generation into older and younger halves. The older Boomers (those born before 1955) were old enough to be drafted into the Vietnam War, to go to Woodstock, and to campaign for George McGovern.[12] They still tend to be more Democratic than the Silent Generation, or even than the younger Boomers, who were too young to experience these formative events in their young adulthood. Older Baby Boomers are more likely to be the parents of Generation X; younger Baby Boomers to be parents of Millennials.

Generation X: This much smaller generation passed its childhood in less optimistic decades than either half of the Baby Boomers had experienced. Their earliest memories were of corruption in government, gasoline shortages, economic stagnation, and gloomy predictions of a coming environmental catastrophe. The oldest GenXers entered young adulthood during the severe recession of the early 1980s. Perhaps because of these factors, they have been stereotyped as cynical and pessimistic, extremely reluctant to trust any institution, whether government, church, or business. The smaller number of GenXers was due to the availability of contraceptive pills to the older half of the Baby Boomers, who had been expected to begin to marry in the late 1960s and produce large families as their parents had done—but who often chose to postpone both of these decisions. GenXers were the first generation in which a large number of their parents were divorced: 45 percent of them were raised either in a family that experienced a divorce or else by a single parent.[13] Many were "latchkey kids" returning from school to an empty house and shunted between their parents on weekends. As they entered their twenties and thirties, many were reluctant to commit themselves to a marriage or a career because they feared that neither would last. Older generations, unsympathetic to their fears, tended to accuse them of "Peter Pan-ishness." Although surveys have shown GenXers to have a higher level of materialistic values than previous generations, they may be the first generation to reverse the historical trend of not earning more (in inflation-adjusted dollars) than their parents did.

The Millennials: In sheer size, this is the largest and most ethnically diverse generation the United States has ever had. In contrast to Gen X "latchkey kids," Millennials were more likely to be welcomed and planned-for "trophy children," some of whose parents were middle-aged Baby Boomers who had spent thousands of dollars in expensive fertility treatments to conceive them. Protected, prodded to achieve, and frequently told how "special" they were when they were children, Millennials are now accused of narcissism, lack of empathy, and an inflated sense of entitlement.[14] Their childhoods were over-planned by adults—75 percent of their time was spent in structured experiences—and employers today complain that they need too much supervision and cannot work independently.[15] Millennials are more likely than the two previous generations to say they are close to their parents—40 percent of Millennial college students phoned, emailed, or texted their parents daily, and another 20 percent contacted them even more often than that.[16] Their "helicopter parents," meanwhile, hover over their young, intervening in problems with their child's professors and even, later, with their child's employers. Accustomed to material prosperity in their childhoods, Millennials are even more materialistic than Generation X. In an annual poll conducted since the early 1960s, 75 percent of Millennials who were freshmen in 2005 said that it was essential or very important for them to be rich, as compared to 62 percent of Gen X freshmen in 1980 or 42 percent of Baby Boomer freshmen in 1966.[17]

On the other hand, Millennials have been less likely to engage in violent crime, teen pregnancy, or alcohol/drug use.[18] They are "digital natives": accustomed to personal computers, email, and cell phones from childhood, they spend more time online than they do watching TV. Millennial college graduates have spent less than five thousand hours of their lives reading, but over ten thousand hours playing video games.[19] On average, young adults spend eleven hours a day on digital media and twenty-three hours each week just texting.[20] Millennials are multitaskers, finding it hard to focus on just one thing for any length of time. Image-driven and nondiscursive, they prefer experience to logic and linear reasoning.

Millennials are the most heterogeneous of the current generations: most report having friends of another race, ethnicity, or sexual orientation. They accept a wide variety of races and lifestyles. In fact, some observers claim that the only things Millennials are not tolerant of is hypocrisy and intolerance! Conscious of their own diversity, they often resist being lumped together under a single generational label. They are "postmodern" in their thought patterns, suspicious of any person or organization that claims there is a single truth that is true for everyone. They are more likely to say that there are many different, even contradictory, truths—they may readily say that something is "true for me" but strongly resist saying it is independently true for everyone.[21]

The Great Recession hit Millennials especially hard: only 54 percent were in the workforce in 2011, the smallest percentage ever for that age group.[22] Their unemployment rate is twice as high as that of other adults, and those who were employed in 2008 experienced the largest drop in earnings of any age group. Possibly as a result of their dismal job prospects, more have remained in, or returned to, college. They are one of the most educated generations in history: 18 percent have a bachelor's degree, as compared to 16 percent of Generation X and barely 11 percent of Baby Boomers.[23] But this extra education has not paid off as well as they had expected, and it also piles up more college debt: 90 percent have significant indebtedness by the time they graduate (if, indeed, they graduate at all—since many fail to complete college due to financial pressures). The average debt load for Millennial college students at graduation was $27,000 in 2013.[24]

As a result of their debts and poor employment prospects, almost one-third (31 percent) have postponed marriage and having children; 24 percent of white and Hispanic Millennials have moved back with their parents.[25] And yet, the basically positive worldview they developed in their 1990s childhoods has not changed: they remain extremely optimistic about their own and the country's future prospects—far more than their elders are.[26] One author calls Millennials "some of the most optimistic people we have ever encountered when it comes to their own personal lives and futures."[27] They still assume that someday they will have a fulfilling career that "makes a difference" in the world, and they would rather have no job than one they hate.[28] Ninety-one percent of Millennials expect that they will, on average, stay in any given job for less than three years.[29] Meanwhile, many have filled the hiatus between school and work with volunteering: after the first class of Millennials graduated from college, the applications for the Peace Corps went up 80 percent, and the applications for Teach for America went up 40 percent. Both organizations have seen a steady rise in participants, to a forty-year high in 2010.[30] Other Millennials have begun their own businesses: more than 40 percent want to found their own company, and almost a third of all US entrepreneurs today are Millennials.[31]

The "Post-Millennials": September 11, 2001, was a crystallizing event that has shaped, and will shape, both the Millennials and the generation following them. Most of this as-yet-unnamed subsequent generation is still in middle school or high school, and the oldest are only now beginning to reach young adulthood. They have grown up in a very different atmosphere from the Millennials' relatively peaceful 1990s childhood: most cannot remember a time when the economy was good, or when the United States was not threatened by terrorism. Some observers fret that, like Generation X, Post-Millennials are growing up deprived of their parents' attention—this time because their parents are avid social media users, tweeting and texting their own friends or business associates when their children want to talk to them.[32]

While Millennials had tended to evaluate their own abilities and the country's future positively, their successors are less sanguine. One author, herself a member, has labeled this generation "Cynic Kids," and says they dislike the present state of affairs in this country but distrust the alternatives.[33] They are troubled by the widening gap between the wealthy and everyone else, especially since they have little hope of ever being wealthy themselves. Communications technology has had a larger impact on this new generation than it had even on the Millennials, who used a personal computer at home and a cell phone only to stay in voice contact with their helicopter parents. The Post-Millennial generation carry their smart phones with them at all times and are more likely to use them for instant messaging, Snapchat, tweeting, Pinterest—the list goes on. These omnipresent electronic gadgets have affected Post-Millennials' ability to communicate with those who don't use such devices. One critic notes that the teens she studied were actually afraid to talk on the phone and didn't know how to conduct a face-to-face conversation.[34] Millennials worry about Post-Millennials, "who haven't yet formed a solid web of real-life relationships or learned how to function in a meat-space (that is, a real-life) social environment."[35] Post-Millennials may, these critics fret, end up socially and emotionally stunted for the rest of their lives. They are used to being constantly connected and experience extreme anxiety if separated from their devices: having grown up in a culture preoccupied with terrorism, they do not assume they will be safe. Their phone represents security to them.[36]

These brief descriptions touch only the surface of each generational culture. Numerous books have been written about the Baby Boomers and the Millennials, and, to a lesser extent, about the Silent Generation and Generation X. But even this cursory overview should be enough to give the reader an impression of how very different these generational cohorts are from each other in the cognitive and value aspects of their cultures. These differences will be important when we discuss the way each generation views Catholicism.

A Digression on Ethnic Generations

If members of different age cohorts of native-born Americans have experienced such different environments as they grew up, we can easily imagine how different the experiences of the children of immigrant parents have been. The "Second Generation" of any ethnic group are the persons born in the United States to parents who had immigrated here as adults. The term "Third Generation" refers to persons whose parents were born in the United States but whose grandparents were immigrants.[37]

Second Generation children and young adults straddle two cultures. As young children, they first learn their parents' language and the cognitive and value aspects of their parents' culture. Once they begin school, however, they are exposed to the same American culture as their classmates, with all of its particular generational influences. Navigating between the two is often difficult. Some children, to fit in, reject their parents' culture and refuse to speak their parents' language.[38] Others, especially teenagers, develop their own hybrid culture, opposed to both their parents' old worldviews and the values of mainstream America. Still others simply feel lost, as though they don't really fit in anywhere. The Third Generation, in contrast, usually has fewer conflictual feelings about whether they belong in America.[39] This generation, secure in its "American" identity, may be intrigued by their grandparents and try actively to relearn what their Second Generation parents had rejected.

Conclusion

Generations are cultures, as distinct in many ways as ethnic cultures are within the United States. And each generation contains within it a plurality of different ethnic and class subcultures. Or, to put it the other way, each ethnic group or social class has generational subcultures. Each of these subcultural groups is likely to view key aspects of American society differently from groups with a different combination of ethnic, class, and generational cohort influences. One of the aspects that they will view differently is American religion and the various churches and denominations in which religion is enacted.

Because each subculture has different cognitive, value, and behavioral aspects, specific denominations have often appealed to just one group. There are working-class, middle-class, and upper-class denominations, each with fundamentally different ways of worship.[40] There are predominantly African American, Hispanic, Asian, and White American denominations.[41] There are even churches whose members are largely from one generational cohort. While, on the one hand, such denominations can be very successful in reaching out to their targeted population, they are less successful at attracting others. And this can become a real problem for ethnic denominations when the second- and third-generation children and grandchildren come along, or with any increasingly aging church that no longer appeals to younger generational cohorts.

But the Catholic Church, by its very name, is to be "universal." We are called to speak the Good News "to all nations," in the language that each can understand. So we first have to learn these languages—the particular and unique way each ethnic group, each social class, and each generation views the Great Questions of life, how (and whether) each envisions God, and the needs each has for the church to meet. Exploring generational differences in Catholics is the task of the next chapter.

5

Generational Cultures in the US Catholic Church

"I will maintain my covenant between me and you and your descendants after you throughout the ages."

—Genesis 17:7

How have the different generations outlined in the previous chapter experienced the Catholic Church? What were the childhood experiences and the crystallizing events of their young adulthood that have shaped their Catholic identity and practice today? In addition to the events that affected all the members of their generation, US Catholics were exposed to additional formative influences that shaped their cohort's worldview, including, most especially, the Second Vatican Council. Catholics who experienced the changes of Vatican II after they became adults, Catholics who experienced them as they were entering adulthood, and Catholics who do not even remember the pre-Vatican II church will all have different attitudes about the beliefs and practices involved in being "Catholic" today. Catholic researchers have slightly altered the standard generational categories listed in the previous chapter to take into account the seminal impact of the council on the different age cohorts of American Catholics, and this book will do the same.[1]

Generational Cultures of American Catholics

While the Second Vatican Council had a profound impact on theology, liturgy, ecumenism, and many other aspects of Catholicism, this book is primarily concerned with its impact on the different generational cultures in the US church today. The council's changes may not be the primary cause of generational shifts in American Catholicism: the gradual assimilation of third- and fourth-generation Catholic ethnic groups to mainstream American culture undoubtedly played a greater role, as did the unique and cataclysmic events of the 1960s in general. But the Conciliar *aggiornamento* opened the American church's windows to these larger societal changes, and gave US Catholics permission to participate in them. The result was a very different kind of Catholic culture—for good and for ill—among those who came of age during and after Vatican II, as compared to the culture of their parents and grandparents. To see how different, we must first discuss the pre-Vatican II generation.

The Pre-Vatican II Generation: Born before 1943

This generation of Catholics includes most of the Silent Generation, plus any remaining members of the Greatest Generation. They are the last to have passed both their childhood and their early adulthood within an all-encompassing Catholic subculture. Especially in the Northeast, Middle Atlantic, and Midwestern states, a large proportion of them attended parish schools, were taught almost entirely by religious sisters, and had little contact with non-Catholics. The vast majority are non-Hispanic whites, descended from the great European waves of Catholic immigrants in the nineteenth and early twentieth centuries.

But even for those who are three or more generations removed from this immigrant experience, Catholicism was in the very air they breathed, in much the same way that it was in the home villages of today's immigrants from Latin America. This pervasive Catholic environment fundamentally shaped the cognitive and value aspects of their Catholic identity in a way that has resisted change ever since. To this day, surveys show that pre-Vatican II Catholics have a measurably stronger affiliation with their religion than Mainline Protestants the same age have to theirs, and much stronger ties to Catholicism than subsequent Catholic generations have. Between one-half and two-thirds have consistently attended Mass weekly or more often for the past twenty-five years, and 41 percent say they are "highly committed" to the church.[2] Pre-Vatican II Catholics also score highest on other measures of Catholic identity. For example, they are by far the most likely of any Catholic generation to watch religious television (42 percent report doing so), or to read religious books and periodicals. Few can imagine ever leaving Catholicism for another religion.

The importance of this pervasive Catholic culture in transmitting a strong religious identity and worldview can be seen by comparing the pre-Vatican II generation with younger age cohorts who did not experience this culture to the same extent, if at all. There has been a sharp drop-off in religious commitment between the pre-Vatican II generation and all of the subsequent generations of Catholics: twice as many pre-Vatican II (41 percent) as younger generations (16–20 percent) are highly committed Catholics.[3] This is by far the steepest cross-generational decline of any Christian denomination in the United States. While the pre-Vatican II generation outscored both Mainline and Evangelical Protestants in the strength of their religious affiliation, the youngest generation of Catholic adults now rank *lower* than their peers in these other denominations.[4] The impact of absorbing a pervasive Catholic culture in childhood does attenuate somewhat in adulthood, especially in those exposed to more secular environments. Even for the pre-Vatican II generation, there has been a decline in religiosity: twice as many (35 percent) seldom or never attend Mass today as compared to this generation's percentage twenty-five years ago (18 percent).[5] They have also expressed a gradually increasing reluctance to give sole authority to church teachings on divorce, contraception, abortion, and homosexuality.[6] These life-cycle effects, however, are less powerful than the cohort effect of having been raised in an all-encompassing Catholic culture that subsequent generations often did not experience.

The Vatican II Generation: Born 1943–1960

The Vatican II generation includes most of the Baby Boomers, plus the youngest of the Silent Generation. The defining characteristic of this generational cohort is that its members experienced the changes of Vatican II prior to or while entering young adulthood. Like the Baby Boomers who comprise most of this age cohort, the Vatican II generation could be divided into older and younger halves. The older Vatican II Catholics passed their childhood in the same kind of all-encompassing Catholic culture experienced by the pre-Vatican II generation, and they have early memories of the Latin Mass, the *Baltimore Catechism*, parochial schools with only religious sisters as teachers, and Catholic devotions such as May Crowning, Forty Hours, etc. Those who were born after 1955 are less likely to remember these experiences. The older members of the Vatican II generation, therefore, experienced as teenagers the changes that followed the council, and found them to be exciting and liberating when compared to the more traditional Catholicism of their childhood. They enthusiastically embraced guitar Masses and more "relevant" religion classes, and many also began to participate in social justice activities such as the United Farm Workers boycotts or the rallies for peace during the

Vietnam War. Even today, it is the older half of the Vatican II generation that is disproportionately represented in organizations such as Pax Christi, Voice of the Faithful, or Call to Action. Because they had experienced being surrounded by a Catholic culture in their childhood—however stultifying they may later have defined it as being—they are more likely to remain Catholic and exercise their "voice" for change than they are to "exit" the church.[7]

Several of the cultural changes that would become more evident in subsequent generations began with the Vatican II generation. There was an abrupt drop-off in Mass attendance between the pre-Vatican II and the Vatican II generations, but only a gradual decline thereafter.[8] Both the Vatican II and later generations of Catholics are barely half as likely as the pre-Vatican II Catholics to agree that the Catholic Church is the "One True Church," and twice as likely to believe that women should be ordained.[9] The Vatican II generation of American Catholics is the first generation to make the distinction between being "spiritual" and being "religious" and the first to evince a sharp decline of trust in the institutional church.[10] The younger members of this generation begin to resemble subsequent generations in being more likely to "exit" Catholicism if they are dissatisfied, and less likely to remain and exercise their "voice" for change.[11]

The Post-Vatican II Generation: Born 1961–1981

This generation is roughly coterminous with Generation X in secular literature. Catholics in this generational cohort received their entire religious formation in the post-Vatican II era. Unlike the previous generations, they had no experience of an all-encompassing Catholic environment to form their religious identity. By the time they were in grade school, the *Baltimore Catechism*, with its rote memorization, had been discarded in favor of more experiential religious education. Fewer members of this generation attended parochial schools, and few, if any, sisters taught them there. Distinctively Catholic devotions such as May Crowning, Forty Hours, and Benediction had been de-emphasized. "[T]he old system of Catholic faith transmission—which relied on concentrated Catholic residential neighborhoods, ethnic solidarity, strong Catholic schools, religious education designed to reinforce family and parish life, and 'thickly' Catholic cultures, practices, and rituals—had drastically eroded . . . yet no alternative approach to effective intergenerational Catholic faith transmission had been devised" to replace it.[12]

The post-Vatican II generation's experience of the church was often of an institution in constant and disorienting flux, unable to articulate anything worth believing in. While nineteenth-century Catholics had struggled with the question of what it meant for them to be *American*, the post-Vatican II generation had to figure out what it meant for them to be *Catholic*.[13] Like the younger members of the Vatican II generation, they are deeply suspicious of all institutions, including religious ones, believing them to be predominantly concerned with obsolete rules, with little to say about the world's most pressing problems.[14] Most post-Vatican II Catholics remain relatively uninformed about religious history or church teachings and consider religion irrelevant, preferring an eclectic, do-it-yourself spirituality. They are only half as likely as the Vatican II generation, and less than one-third as likely as the pre-Vatican II generation, to say it is important to obey church teaching they do not understand or agree with.[15] Contrary to the pattern of previous generations, most of the post-Vatican II generation have not returned to regular religious practice after they married and began their families.[16]

The Millennials: Born since 1982

Millennials are two or more generations removed from pre-Vatican II Catholicism. Most have parents from the younger members of the Vatican II generation or from the older members of the post-Vatican II generation, both of whom had had little or no experience with the traditional Catholic practices and catechesis that had formed previous age cohorts. Fewer than 10 percent of Millennial Catholics have ever attended Catholic schools.[17] How have these differences affected their Catholicism?

In 2005, a major national study charted the religious and spiritual lives of American teenagers.[18] The study was based on a survey of teens from all Christian denominations, plus other religions such as Judaism, Buddhism, Islam, and Mormonism, and was supplemented by 267 in-depth, face-to-face separate interviews of teens and their parents. Of all the various religious backgrounds covered in the book, however, only Catholic teens had an entire chapter devoted solely to them. When he was asked why this was so, the senior author of the book said it was because the Catholic teens uniformly scored lower than all other Christian teens (and much lower than Mormon teens) on every measure of religiosity the researchers measured. The National Conference of Catholic Bishops was so disturbed by this finding that it reprinted the study's chapter on Catholic teens and distributed it through its website. Are Catholic Millennials really that bad?

The reality is a bit more nuanced. *All* Millennials have been disproportionately likely to abandon religious affiliation when they became adults: 33

percent claim to have "no religion" today, as compared to only 12 percent of young adults in the 1970s.[19] This is most likely because of the negative impressions Millennials had received during their 1990s childhoods, of intolerant Christian political activists trying to impose their narrow beliefs on the country as a whole.[20] Millennials in general also objected to Christians' "swagger," judgmentalism, and excessive certainty. One study found that 38 percent of Millennials have a "bad impression" of present-day Christianity.[21] Some studies find that Catholic Millennials have a defection rate that is similar to the rest of their generation: while 20 percent of college-age Millennials today say they are Catholic, another 8 percent say that they *used* to be Catholic in childhood but no longer are, "indicating a significant drop-off of Catholic affiliation by adulthood."[22] Others say Catholic Millennial defection rates are even worse than Millennials of other denominations: one author calls it "eye-opening."[23] On the other hand, critics of this pessimistic view note that seven in ten Catholic young adults still remain affiliated with their faith in some way, a higher proportion than any other Christian faith group except Greek Orthodox.[24] Catholic Millennials are also less likely than Protestant youth to become atheists when they enter adulthood.

But while many Millennials do remain Catholic in name, they are, by and large, only marginally attached to their faith. At least half strongly agree that they are proud to be Catholic, but more than one-third rarely or never attend Mass; another third do so only a few times a year.[25] Most do not believe that missing Mass is a sin. They are the least likely of all Christian young adults to pray once a day or more, to say that they believe in God, or to claim that their faith is "very" or "somewhat" important in shaping their daily life.[26] They are less active in their parishes, least likely to attend religious education sessions, least likely to be part of a youth group, prayer group or choir, and least likely to have talked with their priest or to have adult friends in their congregation.[27] Fewer than a quarter accept the church's teaching authority on moral issues such as divorce, contraception, abortion, homosexuality, and nonmarital sex.[28] Millennial and post-Vatican II Catholics are less than half as likely as Protestants their age to say that the Bible or religious leaders have "a great deal" of influence on how they think about money, and the percentage of materialistic freshmen is actually higher at Catholic colleges than it is at nonreligious or at evangelical colleges.[29] Most importantly, Millennial Catholics are among the least likely to think that it is important to marry another Catholic, and the most likely to say that they will probably not be attending a Catholic church in ten years.[30] A far larger percentage of Millennial Protestants (22.9 percent) than Millennial Catholics (6.4 percent) claim to be "very religious"; in fact, half of the Catholics in one survey said they would actually be embarrassed to be thought "too" religious.[31]

For the most part, however, Millennial Catholics are not—yet—*anti*religious. Instead, their primary attitude toward religion is a sort of benign neglect. The original 2005 survey's authors label this attitude a kind of "Moralistic Therapeutic Deism," whose main tenet is that religion exists to make people feel good about themselves but that it does not, and *should* not, play an important role in everyday life.[32]

As befits the most heterogeneous generation the United States has ever had, however, Millennial Catholics display a wide range of variation in their beliefs and practices. Numerous writers have advanced typologies purporting to describe these variations.[33] Whatever the number and the labels attached to these categories are, however, all agree that few Millennial Catholics fall into the most religiously connected category. According to one estimate, only 2 percent are "devoted" Catholics—attending Mass weekly or more, praying at least a few times a week, feeling close to God, and saying that their faith is very important in their life.[34] This is the lowest percentage of any faith or Christian denomination that the researchers studied. In contrast, Catholics are more likely than Protestant Millennials to be "sporadic" or "disengaged" members of their religion.[35] Some studies, using somewhat looser criteria, estimate that the rate of "active" young adult Catholics may be as high as 10 or 15 percent.[36] Even this latter figure, however, is only a minority of all Catholic Millennials.

Catholic "Fundamentalists"

The 2 percent of Catholic Millennials who fall into the "devoted" category are a true cognitive minority within their generation's culture. As such, they have often reacted to the egalitarianism, post-modernism, and tolerance of the majority of their generation *by aggressively promoting the exact opposite*:

- Instead of tolerance, they proclaim there is only one way to be a "real" Catholic, and condemn those who do not follow it.
- Instead of egalitarianism, the seminarians among them say that the priesthood is a special and holier state.[37]
- Instead of post-modernism, they proclaim that there is only one truth, and that it is found in the Catholic Church and in strict adherence to the magisterium.

Hayes labels this cognitive minority the "Catholic Fundamentalists." While many Millennial Catholics (10–15 percent) do practice their faith at least somewhat regularly and are even intrigued by the sense of the sacred that they experience in traditional devotions such as Eucharistic Adoration, they are *not* the same as the Fundamentalist 2 percent and may even be repelled by them. This is just fine with the Fundamentalists, who cherish the belief that they are a "pure remnant" and that the less-pure are not *really* Catholic.

> Communities with attitudes of Catholic fundamentalism polarize their members and "outside" those in disagreement with them or with aspects of Catholic tradition . . . . the alarmist tendency is to construct "extreme Catholicism," where believers are a type of "Catholic Taliban" (a term cited by those who form these types of communities—so I use the word not to titillate here), which often serves to alienate more than to construct.[38]

These communities, Hayes says, safeguard the purity of their cognitive culture by isolating themselves from outside influences, confining themselves to "a limited experiential realm that locks them inside a clannish group."[39] As was noted in the preceding chapter, an essential part of the cognitive culture these oppositional minorities create is their relationship with the majority culture—either to shield themselves from it or to actively combat it. One Evangelical Protestant writer, who himself grew up in just such a cultural bubble within his own denomination, wonders "how helpful it was to completely disconnect ourselves from the world's happenings around us. Families like ours who choose to separate from the world do so believing it is the only way to maintain their purity and holiness in a fallen, sinful place. This leads them to interact exclusively within their own circles, thus having very few meaningful relationships with people outside the subculture."[40]

The problem, of course, is that it is disproportionately this 2 percent that is showing up in our seminaries and religious orders. This has, potentially, two extremely negative effects:

- Since the majority of Catholics—of all generations—are *not* becoming more conservative, having an unusually conservative clergy may further alienate them from the church.[41] This is especially true of Catholic Millennial and post-Vatican II women, as will be seen below.

- If the only young people who enter the priesthood or religious life come from this ultra-orthodox cognitive minority, then other young men and women who have vocations, whether to vowed religious life or to lay parish ministry, may ignore God's call because they don't think they would fit in—or because, as true children of their generation, the one thing they are intolerant of is the intolerance of the ultra-orthodox.[42]

So what happens? One recent study has found that, among Protestants, those who are repelled by the self-righteous clannishness of the ultra-religious tend to disaffiliate from religion completely. This leads to a polarization between a smaller but still sizeable religious minority and a larger secular one.[43] In contrast, Catholics, rather than leaving the faith completely, shift to nominal affiliation.[44] Neither reaction is helpful for the health or the growth of the church, or of religion in general.

Ethnicity and Generation in Catholicism ✓

In addition to the ultra-traditionalist cognitive minority, another important segment of Millennial Catholics to consider is Hispanics. A full 54 percent of Millennial Catholics are Hispanic; only 39 percent are non-Hispanic whites.[45] Hispanic Millennials are more likely to agree with the church theological teachings on Christ's resurrection, on Mary as the Mother of God, and on the sacraments. They are also more likely to support its moral teachings on abortion and helping the poor. They are much more likely (86 percent as compared to 68 percent for non-Hispanic Millennials) to say that being Catholic is an important part of their identity, that the sacraments are essential to their relationship with God (86 percent as compared to 67 percent), that Catholicism contains a greater share of the truth than other religions (83 percent as compared to 50 percent), and that it is important to them that the younger generations of their family grow up Catholic (83 percent as compared to 71 percent).[46] And they are much *less* likely than non-Hispanic Millennial Catholics to say that one can be a good Catholic and still disagree with church teachings on abortion (48 percent of Hispanic Millennials as compared to 64 percent of non-Hispanic Millennials), the Real Presence of Christ in the Eucharist (33 percent as compared to 51 percent) or the Resurrection (25 percent as compared to 41 percent).[47]

However, as successive generations of Hispanic Catholics assimilate to American culture, they are beginning more and more to resemble non-Hispanic Catholics in their beliefs.[48] Already, similarly small percentages of Hispanic and non-Hispanic Millennial Catholics (29 percent and 24 percent) agree with the bishops' opposition to same-sex marriage, and a similar plurality (42 percent and 41 percent) say that being able to disagree with church teachings and still be loyal to the church is very meaningful to them.[49] Hispanic Millennial Catholics are disproportionately US-born. What will happen as they assimilate further to US culture? "Much of the Catholic experience in the country during the next few decades will be significantly shaped by how the church reaches out to this group and whether young Hispanics in this age bracket, at least those growing up in Catholic households, decide to self-identify as Catholic."[50]

An example of the difficulties inherent in the assimilation of Catholic ethnic groups to the larger US culture can be seen in several studies of second- and third-generation Korean-American Catholics, most of whose parents and grandparents arrived in this country in the 1960s and 1970s. One study noted that there has been a "silent exodus" of second-generation Korean-Americans, both Catholic and Mainline Protestant, from their parents' congregations to American evangelical churches.[51] Of all second-generation Koreans in this country, 19 percent report having been Catholic in their childhood, but only 11 percent report being Catholic as young adults—and a mere 5 percent are formally affiliated with a parish.[52] The traditional Korean Catholicism of their elders no longer speaks to their own experience. But changing to meet these new needs is often difficult for Korean ethnic parishes. Beyond the logistical difficulty of families juggling attendance at two different liturgies is the deeper problem of devising new cognitive and value cultural narratives of Catholicism that speak to the next generation's experiences. "More than ever Korean Americans are in need of the unspoken narrative to be told in order to understand their presence and purpose in between two worlds."[53] Without such narratives, the native Korean missionaries sent for a three- or four-year stint to minister to Korean Catholics in the United States find it difficult to relate to second-generation Korean-Americans, and Korean-American priests find it difficult to relate to first-generation Korean elders.[54] As long as there is a constant influx of new migrants, the defection of the second generation may be masked. But among ethnic groups such as Korean-Americans, where immigration from the old country has ceased, the older immigrant generation who form the majority of their ethnic Catholic parish will ultimately "fail in the transmission of what is important to them, while the next generation does not have the adequate resources to navigate their lives caught between two worlds."[55]

A similar dynamic may occur among second- and third-generation Hispanic Americans. As they increasingly resemble non-Hispanic Catholics their age, the youngest generation of Hispanic-Americans is less likely to attend Mass regularly, to report praying frequently, or to consider themselves "strong" Catholics or "religious persons."[56] And like the Koreans before them, many are leaving Catholicism for Evangelical churches.

Millennial Catholic Women ✓

Another ominous finding is that alienation from the church is stronger among Catholic young adult women than among their male counterparts.[57] *This is highly unusual.* In the past, Catholic women, like women in all other Christian denominations, have been *more* orthodox in their beliefs and *more* observant in their devotions and Mass attendance than men were. At least since the 1990s, however, these proportions have been reversed for Catholics but not for Protestants. While both genders of Millennial and post-Vatican II American Catholics are far less devout than their elders, *the women are even more alienated than the men.* They are now less likely than men their age to say that the church is an important part in their lives, and slightly less likely to say that they would never leave Catholicism. While, for older generations, women reported attending weekly Mass in greater percentages than the men did (52 percent as compared to 35 percent in 1987), now both genders are equally likely to report a much lower level of attendance.[58] Millennial women are more likely than men their age to disregard official church teaching on contraception, abortion, divorce and remarriage, and same-sex sexual activity, and they are also more likely to say that they can disagree with certain aspects of church teaching and still remain good Catholics.[59]

At the present, this alienation occurs primarily among non-Hispanic Millennial women, who, one study reports, "Stand out for their apparent disengagement from and indifference toward Catholicism."[60] But, as second- and third-generation Hispanic women assimilate to American culture, they may come more to resemble non-Hispanic Catholic women. Like their non-Hispanic sisters, the youngest generation of Hispanic Catholic women do not show significant differences with Hispanic Catholic men in Mass attendance, frequency of prayer, or agreement with church teachings on issues of premarital sex, abortion, or homosexuality.[61]

As one study notes, "that there is a generational split among women on the issue of loyalty and dissent presages the larger, significant shift in women's commitment to the Church. . . . The emergent generation divide among Catholic women suggests that younger women—and Millennial and non-Hispanic women in particular—are not likely to stay within the fold of a church whose sexual teachings and church practices are out of step with their lived experiences."[62] It is likely, these authors state, that the women's alienation will also lead to a decline in the commitment of their husbands and children.[63]

There already is evidence that this is happening. The number of marriages celebrated in the church fell 60 percent between 1972 and 2011—from 415,487 to 165,400.[64] "To put it another way, this is a shift from 6.4 Church-sanctioned marriages per 1,000 U.S. Catholics in 1972 to 2.5 per 1,000 in 2011."[65] This decline is only partially because Millennials are more likely to postpone marriage; it is also due to Catholic Millennials' tendency—especially among the rising percentage of Millennials who marry non-Catholics—to eschew Catholic weddings in favor of rites performed in other denominations, or at more exotic locations such as parks, beaches, or even Disney World. With fewer parents having Catholic-sanctioned marriages, the number of Catholic baptisms has declined as well—both absolutely and in proportion to the number of total births. The percentage of US babies baptized Catholic dropped from a high of 33.9 percent in 1965 to 25.0 percent in 2004, to 20.1 percent in 2011.[66] First Communions have also declined.[67]

Another result of the alienation of Millennial and post-Vatican II Catholic women is their reluctance to engage in church service. According to several recent studies done by the Center for Applied Research in the Apostolate and the National Religious Vocation Conference, there are now, for the first time, fewer women than men who are interested in entering religious orders in the United States.[68] There are also fewer women interested in lay parish ministry.[69] Women are more likely than men to say that parish ministry would not adequately use their gifts and talents. This, too, has implications for the Catholic Church in the future: "Besides the 'vocation crisis' to the priesthood and religious life, there is another crisis of lay vocational workers. The generation of DREs and youth ministers who sprouted up after the Second Vatican Council are now retiring and it is not at all clear who will replace them."[70]

The Challenge—and Promise—of Generational Change

The above summary paints a very discouraging picture of Catholic Millennials' connection to the church. Is it even possible to draw them back? Paradoxically, however, there may actually be more hope precisely *because* they seem so far away. The two ends of any cultural spectrum are often quite close to each other. It is sometimes the individuals—and cultures—that appear to be at the farthest extreme of a particular cultural trait who are the most apt to shift to the exact opposite. For example, the United States routinely registers as one of the most individualistic countries in the world, and yet Americans are also among the most likely to create secular and religious communes. There has never been a time in our history when at least one such group was not present and flourishing here: the Shakers, the Oneida Community, New Harmony, and Zoar, to name only the most well-known.[71] Similarly, a study of a set of West Virginia mountain towns describes how the residents—sturdy, family-oriented, and neighborly in their Appalachian tradition—shifted abruptly to hypochondria, divorce, and mutual suspicion when their area suffered the trauma of a devastating flood.[72]

So perhaps Millennial Catholics are not so hopelessly lost to the church, and so indifferent to its message, as they may seem.

- While Millennial Catholic women are less likely to attend Mass or to claim to be strongly religious than older generations of Catholic women, they continue to equal their elders in their desire to grow closer to God, and in reporting that they have had a life-changing religious experience.[73] So a "God-hunger" still calls to Millennial Catholic women.

- While Millennial and post-Vatican II Catholics know relatively little about their faith, some surveys show that this lack of knowledge bothers them and that they would like to learn more.[74]

- Many Millennial and post-Vatican II Catholics who are not part of the ultra-orthodox, "fundamentalist" minority still value traditional Catholic devotions such as Eucharistic Adoration and the rosary, as well as newer contemplative practices such as Taizé prayer.

- Younger Millennial and Post-Millennial Catholics are deeply troubled by the increasing economic inequality and injustice in the world, and the few who are aware of Catholic Social Justice Teaching are impressed and inspired by it. Many are interested in devoting a year or two to Catholic volunteer programs such as the Jesuit Volunteer Corps.

- The postmodern reluctance of Millennials to say that there is only one truth may deter them from the Catholic Fundamentalists' strict adherence to the magisterium, but the Catholicity of the church, with its wide variety of members and devotional practices, as well as its respect for the findings of science on evolution and global warming, is attractive to them, when compared to Protestant fundamentalist churches.

- In an increasingly individualistic culture, Millennials strongly desire to experience community connection that churches may offer.

There remains a window of opportunity to strengthen these remaining, if tenuous, ties to the Catholic Church among Millennials. But this window is closing. It is by no means certain that the children of the Millennial generation will continue to consider themselves Catholic, if their parents cannot be drawn closer to the church themselves. The next chapter will explore some of the ways this might be done.

6

Welcoming Generational Cultures

"Come, children, listen to me;
  I will teach you fear of the LORD."

—Psalm 34:12

Cultures are always changing; the only static ones are the ones that are extinct. This is true of the various Catholic cultures in our country as well, and of the particular culture(s) of each Catholic parish. A parish that insists on worshipping the same way its members always have—using the same language, singing the same songs, emphasizing the same devotional practices, and calling the same persons to ritual leadership as lectors, cantors, etc.—is failing to heed the Holy Spirit's call in the Acts of the Apostles to speak to each and every person "in his or her own language of the wonderful works of God." Those who do not hear the Gospel preached in their language will leave our parishes and go elsewhere. To the extent that Hispanics are leaving Catholicism for evangelical and Pentecostal churches, to the extent that the Millennial grandchildren of Italian, Irish, German, or Polish immigrants no longer practice the Catholicism of their grandparents—to that extent, our parishes are in danger of lapsing into irrelevance, becoming ever smaller collections of aging participants and, eventually, disappearing altogether. This can't be what the Spirit intended. But how can a parish attract and retain new generations and newly-arriving ethnic groups? What ways have been tried in the past, and how well have they worked?

Hopeful Signs—and Challenges

The first thing to do is to take a clear-eyed view of both the positive and negative aspects of the current situation. On the one hand, a recent study shows that British, American, and Canadian Millennial Catholics are the most likely to have increased their faith practice since 2012 because of the inspiration of Pope Francis—a full 13 percent increase in Mass attendance, for example.[1] A 2013 Gallup Poll found that the previously inexorable rise in those claiming to have no religion at all began to slow in 2012, remaining basically flat from the previous year.[2] Most Millennials are still fairly traditional in the importance that they attach to core Catholic beliefs such as the Incarnation and the redemptive death of Christ on the cross, the role of Mary, and the sacraments. Among the regular Mass attenders (admittedly only a small percentage of their age cohort), Catholic Millennials are equally or even more likely than their elders to assume leadership roles such as lector, greeter, or altar server.[3] While, as the previous chapter noted, Millennial Catholics are less likely to be "strong" or "devout" adherents of their religion than their age peers in other Christian traditions, they are also less likely to have rejected religion completely. There may still be ways, therefore, to draw them back.

On the other hand, the previous chapter also outlined many challenges: attendance at Mass, involvement in a parish, knowledge of and adherence to church teachings, and even willingness to marry and baptize their children in the church have all shown sharp declines from previous generations.[4] The greater alienation of Millennial and post-Vatican II women is especially troubling. And there is evidence that a sharp division exists between an ultra-orthodox Millennial Catholic minority and a relatively lax majority. One survey of Catholic college students and young adults found that their second and third most frequent recommendations for the church's future directions were exactly the opposite of each other: "Go back to tradition; don't water down the faith" compared to "Relate more to modern life."[5] If our parishes are to reach out effectively to such disparate groups, we will need to learn how to speak the Good News in *several* generational "languages."

Reaching Out to the Millennial and Post-Millennial Generations

What are the faith languages that might especially resonate with the Millennial Generation—Catholic young adults in their twenties and thirties for whom pre-Vatican II Catholicism is unremembered ancient history, and whose own culture has been so thoroughly shaped by the internet connectivity of their childhood and adolescence? Despite their different backgrounds and opinions, most young adults have spiritual interests and hungers that the church has a wealth of resources to meet. Some of these hungers are:

- *The burden of "infinite" choices.* While the Vatican II generation may have felt stifled by not having enough choices, Millennials are oppressed by having too many: which college to go to, which career to enter, which person to marry. They tend to put off choosing as long as possible, because to choose one path is to close off others. Few, if any, know of Catholicism's vast treasure in spiritual direction and discernment prayer when making life choices.

- The paradoxical difficulty with *true interpersonal connection* in the digital age. Some researchers have found that spending a lot of time on Facebook can actually make people feel more depressed and isolated. Catholicism already offers a wealth of faith-sharing programs and groups, both general ones like Christ Renews His Parish as well as specific programs like Marriage Encounter and Retrouvaille that are focused on connections between people at particular life stages. More informal opportunities of sharing, such as Theology on Tap or small church groups for young adults, may also be available.

- Opportunities for *quiet* in a buzzing electronic world. One recent experimenter asked some four hundred college students whether they would rather be alone with their thoughts in a bare room for six to fifteen minutes—just sitting quietly in their seats with no phones, books, pens for doodling, or distractions of any kind—or whether they would rather receive a mild but painful electric shock. Two-thirds of the men and one-fourth of the women chose the electric shock rather than being alone with their thoughts.[6] Such discomfort with quiet, paradoxically, may be precisely why some young people like Centering Prayer, Eucharistic Adoration, and Taizé prayer services so much: they long for quiet, even as they fear it.

- *Busyness and lack of time.* As children, Millennials had 37 percent less unstructured time than previous generations. Over half reported feeling "too tired" and rushed.[7] For many, this has not changed since they became adults. The church's tradition of the Examen of Consciousness, or the more recent practice of Christian Mindfulness, may appeal to their desire to live their lives in a more contemplative manner.

- *Consumerism.* Millennials routinely register as the most materialistic and consumerist of any generation, a possible legacy of having grown up in the relatively prosperous 1990s. As with the preceding two characteristics in this list, the tension created by this extreme consumerism may be precisely what makes the opposite attractive. The Franciscan spirituality of poverty and decluttering oneself of possessions may speak to the oppression of having too much "stuff."

These and many other treasures, old and new, in our faith could be exactly what Millennials are hungry for. But such resources will first need to be presented in a language that speaks to *them*. Some Millennial and Post-Millennial Catholics may prefer that their parish offer these treasures in different formats than the church has offered them in the past. Studies have found that young adults generally prefer:

- *Experientially-oriented worship* rather than doctrine, nonlinear thinking in preference to logic in catechesis, media presentations instead of sermons. They may be attracted by the sacred suspension of time they experience in Gregorian chant, incense, and Eucharistic Adoration—or in lively and ecstatic modern liturgies—and less interested in intellectual explications of the faith.[8]

- *Sophisticated electronic outreach* instead of printed books and magazines.

- *Strong community connections.* They need to feel welcomed in a parish, and will rapidly desert any congregation if they do not feel welcomed and at home there.[9]

- *Social activism and volunteering.* This is especially the case as the gap between the rich and the poor in this country becomes more and more evident and troubling. Millennials and Post-Millennials, especially, appear to be suspicious of government efforts to solve these problems, and more sanguine about the beneficial effects of volunteering. But they often do not connect these volunteer experiences with Catholic or Christian spiritual life.

In contrast, most Millennial Catholics will *not* be attracted to any parish or parish group that seems to imply that there is only one way to be Catholic. This may be a parish where long-standing members squelch new ideas because "We've always done it *this* way." Or it may be a parish founded for a particular ethnic group, whose children are no longer comfortable worshipping in Korean or Polish, or where the young are expected to defer to their elders in parish decisions. Or it may be a new pastor from the ultraorthodox minority. Without much cultural attachment to a Catholic parish to begin with, Millennial Catholics will have no reason to put up with a pastor—even a pastor their own age—who demands that everyone must believe and obey everything the church's magisterium decrees, attend Mass weekly, or correct the behavior of their gay friends.[10] They will be equally repelled by "angry" Vatican II Catholics who appear to spend all their time griping about those terrible young conservative priests. Coming from a postmodern peer culture in secular society, Catholic Millennials are reluctant—even more reluctant than others their age—to say that there is only one right way to do something, and they are loath to judge others who think or act differently from how they themselves think and act.[11] They are also strongly egalitarian, and most are strongly offended by church practices that seem to relegate women and gays to second-class status. One Evangelical Protestant author, himself a Millennial, notes that nearly nine out of ten young adults who are not affiliated with a church (and over half even of young adult Evangelical Protestants) think that Christians are too judgmental: "They are arrogant about their beliefs, *but they never bother figuring out what other people actually think.* They don't seem to be very compassionate, especially when they feel strongly about something."[12] Whatever methods or spiritual treasures we decide to use to invite Millennial Catholics to our parishes, therefore, we will need to be aware that *how* we invite them is as important as the treasures we are inviting them *to*.

Recommendations

So what is a parish (or a diocese, or the US Catholic Church as a whole, for that matter) to do? In American religious history, there have traditionally been two models or templates for passing on a faith tradition to the next generation: a "voluntaristic" model that relied on persuading individuals to personally commit themselves to their faith tradition as adults and then to become actively involved in a local congregation of their choice; and a "cultural" model, in which the faith tradition was imbibed in the very air one had breathed from childhood on. Nineteenth- and early twentieth-century Protestants tended to follow the first model, while the Catholic immigrants to the United States tended to follow the second (albeit with increasing borrowings from the "more American" voluntaristic model as the second and third generations assimilated to American life).

Today, however, both models may need revision if they are to be successful in attracting or retaining Millennial and Post-Millennnial Catholics. The voluntaristic model has degenerated, in many cases, to a "consumer mentality," in which "the Church itself has become a commodity. It is one other thing that I can choose to include in my life. Within such a consumer mentality, faith becomes radically diluted."[13] But the second model is also problematic. It is difficult, if not impossible, to construct the kind of all-encompassing religious cultures that once surrounded our immigrant for-bearers. The few attempts to do so—largely by Catholic ultraconservatives or fundamentalist Protestant evangelicals who home-school their children or enroll them in private religious schools, who consume only avowedly Christian or Catholic media, and who openly display other markers of their distinctive identity—simultaneously create in themselves and in their children the sense of being an embattled minority besieged by a hostile majority that is waging a war on their religion.[14] While often successful in passing on the faith to the next generation, this self-consciously beleaguered identity is very different from the "taken-for-grantedness" that had characterized the all-encompassing faith culture of the past. Plus, an embattled cultural version of Catholicism (or of American Evangelical Protestantism) appeals to only a small minority of Millennials.[15]

Is it possible to combine and adapt these two models in some way, so that they might successfully reach out to Millennials and Post-Millennials in all their variety? American Catholicism would seem to be better able to do so than Protestantism or Eastern Orthodoxy, since enfolding a large number of different cultural groups under one faith umbrella—however precariously—has been an important part of our history in this country. We did this once; we should be able to do it again.

First, how might we go about creating and fostering several different Catholic cultural environments for coming generations? One way would be to learn from successful Catholic cultures—past and present. The ethnic parishes of the nineteenth and early twentieth centuries were each "institutionally complete": in addition to Sunday and weekday Masses, they offered a plethora of devotional societies, mutual aid organizations, sports teams, cultural and language preservation classes, devotions for men and women of various different age groups, and, of course, the schools. As one historian put it, "The parish frequently provided an all-embracing or total environment for the religious socialization of its members, with religious, educational, social welfare, and entertainment functions for all circumstances and needs."[16] Many conservative Catholic and Evangelical Protestant Christians today have created similarly complete subcultures. To quote one Evangelical young adult: "So many Christians are caught up in the Christian subculture and are completely closed off from the world. We go to church on Wednesdays, Sundays, and sometimes on Saturdays. We attend small group on Tuesday night and serve on the Sunday school advisory board, the financial committee, and the welcoming committee. We go to barbeques with our Christian friends and plan group outings. We are closed off from the world."[17] But this very encapsulation renders it hard for them to reach out beyond their closed circle. The same Evangelical continues: "Even if we wanted to reach out to non-Christians, we don't have time and we don't know how." Is it possible for Catholic parishes to overcome this encapsulation? For a single parish to foster several, mutually-respecting, generational cultures that learn from and enrich each other while retaining their own distinctive "take" on being Catholic? Or for a diocese to foster "generational parishes" as it once did ethnic ones?

What would a parish with several mutually interacting but distinct sub-cultures—generational, ethnic, theological and/or liturgical—look like? In addition to the traditionalist subcultural version that is already successful within a minority of Catholics,[18] what other variants might appeal to coming generations? In a time when the larger American society is increasingly polarized into red and blue states, liberals and conservatives, Tea Partiers and Occupiers of Wall Street, can the church model a pluralism that is mutually respectful and tolerant of ambiguity and difference—while still remaining true to its basic Catholic identity? Or are we so much a part of our bifurcated society that this is beyond even the Holy Spirit's power?

In contrast to the difficulty that encapsulated cultures have in reaching out beyond their boundaries, the voluntaristic model of passing on the faith to new generations requires that the church's treasures be effectively presented to as wide an audience as possible, so that all listeners can freely and enthusiastically choose them. As St. Paul asks, "How can they believe if they have not heard?" The media for spreading the message today, however, seem to be changing at an ever-accelerating pace. No sooner does a parish awaken to the need to have its own web page (and the need to update said web page on a weekly or even daily basis) than it discovers that its audience now prefers blogs, Facebook, Twitter, Snapchat—the list is endless and endlessly updating. Already email, MySpace, and even Facebook are seen as "yesterday's technology" by the young. And in trying to keep up with the latest fad in communicating our message, are we in danger of the very "commodification" of the Good News that critics have decried? Is offering more and more spiritual options just adding to young adults' already oppressive plethora of choices?

Critics have argued that, instead of adding more options, we need to develop a "vocation theology" to guide and deepen the choices young adults must make. "While the model of choice has its strengths (an emphasis on agency and intentionality, for example), it needs to be placed in the context of God's call. We need a better theology of vocation to show how the spiritual search—so strong among the young—always comes as a response to the loving invitation and uncomfortable challenge that is the call of God."[19] Can developing this theology of vocation—to Christian marriage and single life in the world as well as to the priesthood and religious life—be part of a model that values God's call to one of several different ways of being truly Catholic? How can such a theology be made attractive to—or even come to the attention of—young adults? And how might each of these different ways strengthen and celebrate its own distinct Catholic identity while at the same time respecting the vision of others? The Triune God and this God's "one, holy, catholic, and apostolic Church" are too vast, too alive, and too constantly changing to be confined in one narrow and time-bound representation of Catholicism.

This chapter has already briefly outlined some of the spiritual hungers of Millennial and Post-Millennial Catholics: the burden of too many choices, the search for true interpersonal connection, the lack of times and spaces for quiet reflection, the distractions of busyness, and consumerism. These hungers are the very doors through which our parishes might be able to reach out to marginally connected Catholics and lure them back to fuller participation. The next section will describe some strategies that have been advanced to do precisely that. These strategies will combine both voluntaristic ways of developing practical theologies to aid Millennials and Post-Millennials in choosing how to address their spiritual hungers and also culture-creating ways of fostering the environments that would make these choices easier and more natural for them.

Strategies

To Ease the Burden of Choice

Young adulthood has always been a time for making the choices that will drastically influence one's entire future life. Should I go to college or not? Which college? Which profession should I train for? Whom should I marry? Or should I (gasp!) enter the priesthood or religious life? What city should I/we live in? What house should we buy? When should we start a family?

In the past, making these choices was easier than it is today, paradoxically, *because the range of options was more constrained.* As Americans we tend to assume that having more choices is better, but a moment spent remembering

how many times we have clicked through 150 channels on our cable or sat-
ellite TV, all the while complaining that there was nothing worth watching
on any of them, should disabuse us of that idea.[20] Psychologists have found
that *the more choices we have, the less satisfied we are with any of them.*

> Millennials understand this instinctively. As one of them recently noted,
> "I think the need to close doors has been especially hard for my peers
> and me, who grew up with the message that we could do anything and
> should keep our options open . . . If youth is a time of exploring all
> opportunities and adulthood is for honoring one's commitments, then
> the twenties are when those commitments get made and when some
> opportunities, by necessity, get lost along the way. That's a difficult thing
> to process—and a tempting thing to delay."[21]

Many Millennials, therefore, *do* delay making final commitments: to a per-
manent career path, for example, or to marriage. "They are very often simply
paralyzed, wishing they could be more definite, wanting to move forward,
but simply not knowing how they might possibly know anything worthy of
conviction and dedication."[22] Often, they simply drift into life paths without
actually choosing them, with less than optimal results. Recent research shows
that many young couples have lived together for years but never actually
sat down and *talked* about this decision. "Couples who slide through their
relationship transitions have poorer marital quality than those who make
intentional decisions about major milestones," one researcher notes.[23] But
this is precisely what Millennials resist doing. Some rely on their peers as the
filter for decision-making: "They determine right and wrong based partly on
what makes sense given their experiences and friendships."[24] Others lapse
into "black and white" thinking that "cuts through the process of thinking
about a myriad of choices and makes choice unambiguous. It allows someone
else, who presumably has worked out the answer for you, to provide them on
a silver platter."[25] Having grown up with Google, many Millennials tend to
want instant answers "that are simple, clear-cut, and require little thought."[26]
If such answers are not readily available, they may go back to drifting.

   This chapter has already noted that the church has centuries of experience
with spiritual techniques to address this problem: Ignatian discernment, for
example, or spiritual direction. How might our parishes, schools, and colleges
better acquaint Millennial Catholics with this tradition? On the one hand, the
voluntaristic model would argue that the existence of these resources needs
to be more widely known so that the next generation is able to choose them.
Trained teachers and facilitators in both individual and group discernment

prayer should be available throughout the diocese, and they should offer a wide variety of spiritual discernment activities in our Catholic schools, in our parish youth and young adult groups, on college campuses, online, and in as many other venues and as many age-appropriate formats as can be devised. All this presumes an infrastructure of training and certification programs for the teachers, youth spiritual directors, and facilitators of these programs (perhaps at diocesan seminaries or at the motherhouses of religious congregations), as well as well-developed discernment curricula for all age levels. It presumes ongoing professional development programs and conferences for the discernment program leaders to share which ideas work or don't work. It presumes a readily-available online list of spiritual direction/discernment opportunities and directors. It presumes an effective media effort to make young Catholics facing life choices aware that such discernment resources exist.

On the other hand, all of the efforts to present Catholic traditions of life choice discernment and spiritual direction will be futile—or will degenerate into a "consumerist" watering down of the faith in a desperate attempt to attract more "customers"—without the simultaneous fostering of a truly Catholic culture that encourages a spirituality of life choices. How to create such a culture? From a very early age, Catholic schools might incorporate "praying over" childhood decisions into various aspects of each day. Age-appropriate discernment prayers for parents to say with their children at home might be distributed. Short films might be made to dramatize children, teens, or young adults bringing God into their life decisions, or clips from existing films might be adapted for this purpose. Group spiritual direction sessions might be devised, and regular participation in them expected before confirmation or graduation from a Catholic high school or college, in much the same way that completing a given number of service hours is currently required at these times. Fun activities might be devised at Catholic youth conferences on both the national and diocesan levels to acquaint the participants with discernment practices. All of these are only illustrative (and largely untried) suggestions, meant to give some idea of the kinds of activities that might be initiated in creating a particular Catholic subculture that assumes, and values, spiritual discernment. Other practices could—and should—be devised, and the successful ones shared among parishes and dioceses.

To Encourage Interpersonal Connection

Psychologists have recently begun to worry that our society's many electronic modes of communication are having a detrimental impact on the ability of young people to connect with each other in any depth. Researchers have documented a growing reluctance of teens to talk to each other on the phone because they are unable to edit ahead of time what they say.[27] Having a one-on-one conversation "in the flesh" is even more frightening, as is making eye contact. One author quotes a teen wistfully hoping that maybe he will learn how to have a real conversation "someday."[28] Other writers document a disturbing decline in empathy and a consequent rise in narcissism among the young that they trace to this same reliance on electronic connection, in bursts of 140 characters, without ever needing to see how one's words have affected their recipient.[29] As one teen put it, she gives herself "permission to say mean things" online: "You don't see their reaction or anything and it's like you're talking to a computer screen, so you don't see how you're hurting them. You can say whatever you want, because you're at home and they can't do anything."[30]

If these findings are true, it bodes ill for the psychological and spiritual development of the Post-Millennial generation of Catholics. Our late teens and young adulthood are precisely the time when we are supposed to be navigating Erik Erikson's development stage of "intimacy vs. isolation" by developing adult friendships. And yet, "one thing is eternal about friendship in the twenties: making new friends is hard. Especially if you're shy, especially if you're married, especially if you're in a new city with no easy way to meet people."[31] And especially if you are young in today's job market: "twenty-somethings are more transient than at any other age, and more in need of friendships wherever they happen to land."[32] Young adults are likely to have seven to eight jobs before they enter their mid-thirties, many of which will require moving to an entirely new city or state.[33] They are lonely. Many report feeling an emotional distance from their parents, and not feeling valued by adults in their schools, neighborhoods, or local churches.[34]

And their electronic connection devices may actually be augmenting their loneliness. Simply talking to one other person on the phone or in person feels like a waste of time; it is more efficient to multitask—to participate simultaneously in two or three online chats, surf the net, and update one's own Facebook profile, all at the same time. "Teenagers know that when they communicate by instant message, they compete with many other windows on a computer screen. They know how little attention they are getting because they know how little they give to the instant messages they receive . . . . When you text or instant-message, you have no way to tell how much else is going on for the person writing you. He or she could also be on the phone, doing homework, watching TV, or in the midst of other online conversations. Longed for here is the pleasure of full attention, coveted and rare."[35]

How might our parishes reach out to these hungers for the significant personal relationships that are so foundational for both personal and religious growth? We are, after all, created to know and love God, and we cannot do this if we are unable truly to know and love each other. One author suggests taking advantage of "moments of return" when marginally-connected Catholic Millennials briefly cross our parish doorsteps—the life-cycle events of marriage, baptism, illness, and the death of parents and grandparents—to invite them to interesting-sounding opportunities that might appeal to their hunger for interpersonal connection.[36] We could invite engaged couples planning their marriage in our church to attend social get-togethers and discussion/faith-sharing groups with other newly-married couples, for example, or couples baptizing their infants to a monthly "parents' night out." Alternatively, a parish might imitate the various commercial establishments that, as soon as a new tenant moves into an apartment building, floods his/her mailbox with enticing offers for Wi-Fi services, pizza delivery ads, and coupons for 20 percent off at the local hardware store. If a parish has a program especially geared to young adults—Theology on Tap, for example—such advertising might be a good way to attract newly arrived and uprooted twentysomethings to attend it. A continuous flow of new members into these programs would keep them fresh, lest they become a clique of long-standing regulars whose exclusiveness actually repels new inquirers.[37] A parish or diocese might also make sure that its prayer groups, theological discussion sessions, and social events are listed online and can be readily found on Google or a similar search engine.[38]

True interpersonal relationship is therefore a strong spiritual hunger that the church might foster in some way. Making friends among one's age peers at Catholic high schools and on mission trips has been found to be one of the key factors in preserving their connection with the church as young adults.[39] More such friendship opportunities should be provided. Also important, however, are interpersonal connections *across* generational lines, ongoing and deeply shared relationships between age peers and with older adults who mentor and model what it means to be Catholic today: "New members of any society are always inducted into the group by elder members who form them in different ways to become active participants of various sorts. This is done through role modeling, teaching, taking-things-for-granted, sanctioning, training, practicing, and other means of inculcating and internalizing basic categories, assumptions, symbols, habits, beliefs, values, desires, norms, and practices. This is simply how most youth learn religion and everything else."[40]

Developing such relationships requires intentionality and the sacrifice of one's time and preconceived notions. The evangelical Protestant Millennial author of *UnChristian: What a New Generation Really Thinks about Christianity*, was asked by his pastor-father how to befriend and convert young adults. "Well, yes, relationships are central," the son replied, "but it's not as simple as you think. You don't just 'make friends' with young people, and, bingo, they trust you. You'd have to make a commitment to being a part of their lives, to understanding what makes them tick and how they think . . . It really would be like quitting your job and going overseas to serve as a missionary. You truly immerse yourself in the lifestyles, decisions, relationships, and choices of a completely unique group of people."[41] Both generations will learn from each other in the process.

A necessary part of providing opportunities for this intergenerational learning is to involve young adults in the creation and active leadership of the parish programs we invite them to, instead of considering them merely as passive participants and beneficiaries.[42] As the moderator of the website Busted Halo noted, mutual sharing between the generations is key. "This is not an 'I'll talk and you listen' type of thing."[43] One pastor describes his parish's F.L.A.M.E. program for young adults, an acronym that stands for "Friendship, Leadership, Acceptance, Ministry, and Education." As the name implies, these are opportunities for retreats and for learning more about the faith, as well as social events and service activities. These events are developed and run by members of the targeted age group: "As best we can, we try to make all the ministries involved in F.L.A.M.E. intergenerational, with *peer ministers* assuming leadership in the various ministries, while being mentored in leadership by adults. . . . After confirmation, thirty-five to fifty teens, on average, go on to become peer ministers the following year."[44]

But a single year-long stint as a peer minister is not enough. A pair of researchers recently studied former peer leaders in a retreat program for Catholic middle- and high school students in Canada. They found that these former leaders, now aged seventeen to twenty-six, had had positive experiences in their time as retreat leaders, *but this did not translate into active parish involvement when they became young adults.*[45] Similarly, another author notes that the pervasive Catholic culture of World Youth Day, where "Catholic symbols were everywhere, from the makeshift confessionals where priests heard confessions in an open field all day long, to the beauty and stillness of the evening procession of the Stations of the Cross," dissipated after the event was over.[46] An ongoing and pervasive culture of interpersonal connection is needed to keep the original experience alive.

As with strategies for addressing the Catholic Millennials' surfeit of life choices, addressing their hunger for interpersonal, non-electronically-mediated relationships will require the voluntaristic model's tactics of developing and offering opportunities for such connections within our parishes and dioceses. It will also require the cultural model's tactics of fostering a deep spirit of sharing and community among all the members of our parishes, a culture where new arrivals are welcomed and made to feel at home as soon as they walk in the door.[47] By so doing, we will enrich all generations of our parishioners and, through our mutual love and sharing, grow closer to God.

Quiet, Busyness, and Time Pressures

Many Millennials are also harried and overwhelmed by the noise and the frantic pace of their lives. With fewer good jobs available and with a looming amount of indebtedness from college loans and credit cards, the young adults who are employed feel that they must work longer and harder just to make ends meet. Modern electronic devices make it increasingly difficult for them to "unplug" from their work. "Knowing that employees, especially younger generations, are accessible by email or text at any hour of the day, supervisors are expecting much more from the workforce. There is also a pressure on young adults to go faster because their technology is equally as quick. And even if a supervisor isn't setting such high standards, young adults will often impose a pressure on themselves to check their emails and work from home—just so that they can get ahead of their workload or climb the ladder of success more quickly."[48] These "eclipsed Catholics" may feel that they need to work an extra shift on Sunday. Or they may wish to stay home and spend some quality time with their small children, whose emotional needs they may feel have been neglected during their busy week.[49] They simply don't have the time—or the energy—for going to church or for trying to cultivate a spiritual life. It is easier to passively absorb a distraction from the electronic media devices they constantly carry with them: "These days, when people are alone, or feel a moment of boredom, they tend to reach for a device. In a movie theater, at a stop sign, at the checkout line at a supermarket and, yes, at a memorial service, reaching for a device becomes so natural that we start to forget that there is a reason, a good reason, to sit still with our thoughts."[50] But this author believes that young adults are beginning to realize what this constant connectedness is costing them: "They respond when adults provide them with sacred spaces (the kitchen, the family room, the car) as device-free zones to reclaim conversation and self-reflection."[51]

Can our parishes provide some of these sacred spaces? This will be difficult because the most stressed and overwhelmed Millennial Catholics are the very ones who are too busy to come to church to begin with. Perhaps the only thing we can do to help them is to make simple gestures of presence available. One author suggests offering a spiritual online presence: "On Facebook, keep an eye out for young adults who express stress or frustration and, on these occasions, comment or send a private note of encouragement. On your website consider offering a place where people can click 'Help Me' and interact with a trained spiritual director or supportive minister during challenging times."[52] Another tactic might be to offer a "stress-free zone"—a garden or courtyard or peaceful room that could be an oasis for the overwhelmed. Eucharistic Adoration hours or Taizé prayer services could also provide this kind of quiet oasis: the opportunity to be still is precisely the quality of Eucharistic Adoration that is most often cited by young adults as their reason for attending. Other offerings requiring a bit more of a time commitment on the part of harried young adults might be a "stressed-out support group," spiritual direction for the stressed, or a contemplative prayer night.[53]

Again, of course, merely offering these options is not enough. From earliest childhood a culture has to be fostered that values and supports mindfulness and contemplation. One way to do this might be to offer classes and resources to new parents on being truly present to their children, instead of being tethered to their electronics: "Parents texted with one hand and pushed swings with the other. They glanced up at the jungle gym as they made calls. . . . From the youngest ages, these teenagers have associated technology with shared attention. Phones . . . were the competition, one that children didn't necessarily feel they could best."[54] Developing a culture of contemplation might also mean building quiet reflection times into the school day or after-school activities. It might mean "nature moments" when parents sit quietly with their children to watch a sunset or listen to the birds in the backyard. It certainly would mean extending the retreat opportunities a parish or school offers to children and teens, as well as to young adults. Older adults might be invited to talk to teens and children about how they spent their days in a pre-internet world, and they might be asked to teach kids some of the games they played. The important thing is to foster a culture of quiet, mindfulness, and contemplation among all parish members.

Other Hungers

The hungers mentioned in this chapter are only a small sampling of the doors through which Catholic Millennials could be invited and welcomed into our parishes. Other hungers may be more prevalent in different situations. The consumerist mentality of young adults—almost two-thirds believe that buying more things would make them happier—will inevitably disappoint them. They may then be receptive to retreats or self-help groups centered on a Franciscan spirituality of "de-cluttering" their lives. Young adult searchers may benefit from a "Thomas Ministry" that addresses "Doubting Thomases" who are struggling with their faith.[55] Second-generation Hispanics may seek help in straddling the world of their immigrant parents and the world of American young adults, and may feel out-of-step in either. Gay teens, with their significantly higher rates of depression and suicidal thoughts, certainly need help and care. Teens who are bullied, young adult women in abusive or unhealthy relationships, college students trying to resist (or recover from) the lures of campus sex and alcohol—are all our neighbors. We are deficient in our Christianity if we do not reach out to them as the Samaritan in Christ's parable did: "Go and do likewise."

Conclusion

"Lord, let our eyes be opened."

—Matthew 20:33

In discerning how best to invite different cultural groups, whether ethnic or generational, into our parishes, it might be wise to recall the humorous fable of the six blind men and the elephant that was mentioned in chapter 2. Just as the blind men, each feeling only a part of the elephant, came away with only a partial idea of what the animal actually was, so also we, seeing "indistinctly, as in a mirror" (1 Cor 13:12), have only a partial realization of the "breadth and length and height and depth" (Eph 3:18) of God's love as it is revealed in the church—which, after all, is the Mystical Body of Christ, "and [we are] individually parts of it" (1 Cor 12:27). We impoverish our vision of the Spirit's plan for the church if we limit it to what *we* "see" and ignore the equally valid vision the Spirit has given to other cultural groups.

This pluralism is not the same as trying to make Catholicism "trendy," abandoning its unique treasures and embracing secular fads in order to appeal to picky religious customers. That would be like the blind men abandoning their efforts to understand the elephant and going off to share a drink at the nearest bar instead. But it is, admittedly, difficult at times to know how to modify our liturgies, our theologies, our devotional practices, and our parish governance in a way that preserves the essence of our Catholic identity (the "elephant," so to speak) while simultaneously speaking to the experiences of those we are inviting to join us (is the odd shape that other blind person feels *really* a part of our elephant?). This will take a lot of prayerful discernment, and we will inevitably make mistakes. No human language, no symbol, no way of celebrating the liturgy, no devotional practice, no theology is adequate to encompass the full mystery of God's dealings with us in the church—and this includes the language, symbols, liturgy, and devotions we ourselves are currently using. (For that matter, is what *we* are feeling really part of our elephant? Oh, dear . . .) Yet the Spirit has chosen, for reasons we will never fully comprehend, to entrust the proclamation of the reign of God to the multitude of fallible human languages, symbols, and cultures that have existed throughout the world and across all the centuries since the apostles first left the upper room.

One thing we can be sure of, however: it is not now, and never was, part of God's vision that we waste our time arguing over whose vision is the sole correct one. This is the exact opposite of what the Spirit intended. Jesus showed this in his reactions to his contemporaries: the persons he condemned were not the prostitutes, tax collectors, political radicals, or demon-possessed who came to him, but the Pharisees who preached that *their* way of being Jewish was the only way. Similarly, St. Paul reserved some of his most biting criticisms for those who demanded that his Gentile converts adhere to all the traditional practices of Judaism. It may in fact be true that some of the adaptations people make go beyond the truth of the Gospel—Paul's letters also contain a lot of warnings about false practices and teachings—but any challenging of what we perceive to be incorrect versions of the "elephant" must be done in love and gentleness, and leavened by an honest willingness to be challenged in return by the vision of those we are challenging.

Studies of young people seem to confirm that they are seeing truly different, but real, versions of Catholicism:

> [T]hose who advocate change are not advocating change in the core teachings of Catholicism. When we read the words of these young adults, we hear a call for more dynamic liturgies, better music, relevant messages, less guilt, and more flexibility—not a radical rejection or basic dismissal of the faith. In the same way, those young adults who want to return to tradition are also concerned more with the periphery than with the core of Church teaching. Rather than lively liturgies, they emphasize reverence at Mass, celibacy for priests, and the need for conservative practices like adoration and the use of Latin.[1]

This is less a debate about which is the one true version of the faith than it is a groping toward how to "do" Catholicism in one's everyday life. Similarly, the different ethnic groups we welcome to our parishes have their own ways of "doing" Catholicism—ways we might learn from to enrich our own. Tolerating, even celebrating, such differences in the way our faith is lived out in daily life is likely to be especially attractive to Catholic Millennials of all ethnic backgrounds. And it will also be a prophetic rebuke to our increasingly polarized secular culture.

We are each called to begin this kind of welcoming, this kind of sharing. For some of us, it will mean working to initiate some of the suggestions in the previous chapters to make our parishes more diverse and welcoming to ethnic and generational cultures. For others, it will involve addressing the generational diversity in our own families. One recent study of intergenerational faith transmission found that families from the religious groups that have had the most success in passing on their beliefs and practices—Mormons, Evangelical Christians, and Orthodox Jews—had several common characteristics:

- The families had strong and intentional bonds with their church or synagogue, such that the latter's religious activities were built around family activities, and the family had a high involvement in religious education.
- The parents modeled a strong and active involvement in their religious traditions, beliefs, and practices.
- There was a strong value given to family solidarity, "characterized by warm emotional relationships, frequent family interaction, help, and assistance."[2]

These beneficial familial practices, however, could be nullified if the children experienced an atmosphere of parental religious intolerance or hypocrisy, either with too much and too strict religious socialization or with parents following the letter but not the spirit of the law.[3]

In passing on the faith, the study found that grandparents have a key role as well. Grandfathers, especially, influence the frequency and intensity with which their grandchildren practice their religion. Grandparents who visibly practice the time-honored rituals of Catholicism and invite their grandchildren to join them, grandparents who bear witness to the peace and joy they derive from their religious practice, may have a profound influence on their grandchildren that they do not expect. This is especially the case when the grandparent is a first-generation member of an immigrant ethnic group, witnessing to a third-generation grandchild whose parents have discarded their faith along with the other trappings of the old country.

Parental, and grandparental, efforts will come to naught, however, without the support of welcoming parishes that assist them in these efforts: without support groups, prayer services, spiritual mentoring, social gatherings, and other forms of assistance for second-generation Hispanic teens torn between two cultures, for young adults discerning among a plethora of life choices, for young married couples and new parents, for the frazzled and harried of all ages seeking space for quiet contemplation, for lonely new arrivals—for the whole gamut of human needs our church has a history, and a continuing call, to address. If the current parish staff has neither the time nor the resources to begin all of these initiatives, it should invite the targeted groups themselves to begin them. A special effort should be made to call young women to leadership in these initiatives. Most efforts may fail. But our God—who appeared to end his earthly life with a pretty big failure Himself—doesn't require that we never fail. God only asks that we proclaim the Good News to every people and nation as best and as often as we can. The Spirit will take care of the rest.

Notes

Introduction—(pages 1–10)

1. Karl Mannheim, "The Problem of Generations," in *Essays in the Sociology of Knowledge* (New York: Oxford University Press, 1952), 298.

2. William Biernatzki, *Roots of Acceptance: The Intercultural Communication of Religious Meanings* (Rome: Ediciones Pontificia Universita Gregoriana, 1991), 78, 83.

Chapter 1: Ethnic Groups in the Catholic Church— Past and Present—(pages 11–24)

1. Figures for this paragraph were taken from the entries for Irish, German, Polish, and Italian immigration in *The Encyclopedia of American Catholic History* (Collegeville, MN: Liturgical Press, 1997).

2. Statistics taken from Mark M. Gray, ed., *Nineteen Sixty-four* (blog), Center for Applied Research in the Apostolate at Georgetown University, http://www .nineteensixty-four.blogspot.com/2013/12/mexican-ancestry-more-common -than-any.html.

3. Kathleen Neils Conzen, "German Catholics in America," in *The Encyclopedia of American Catholic History*, 580.

4. James S. Pula, "Polish Catholics in America," in *The Encyclopedia of American Catholic History*, 1144. As Table 1.1 states, an even larger number—6,076—offered religious services in at least one foreign language.

5. Roger Finke and Rodney Stark, *The Churching of America 1776–1990* (New Brunswick, NJ: Rutgers University Press, 1992), 127.

6. Pula, "Polish Catholics in America," 1142.

7. Joseph J. Casino, quoted in Finke and Stark, *The Churching of America*, 127.

8. Lawrence J. McCaffrey, "Irish Catholics in America," in *The Encyclopedia of American Catholic History*, 698.

9. Janice Farnham and Bruce Bradley, "French Canadian Catholics in the United States," in *The Encyclopedia of American Catholic History*, 551.

10. Pula, "Polish Catholics in America," 1148.

11. Conzen, "German Catholics in America," 578.

12. Finke and Stark, *The Churching of America*, 133.

13. Ana Maria Diaz-Stevens, *Oxcart Catholicism on Fifth Avenue: The Impact of the Puerto Rican Migration upon the Archdiocese of New York* (Notre Dame, IN: Notre Dame University Press, 1993), 73.

14. Quoted in Stephen J. Shaw, "The Cities and the Plains, a Home for God's People: A History of Catholic Parish Life in the Midwest," in *The American Catholic Parish: A History from 1850 to the Present,* ed. Jay P. Dolan (New York: Paulist, 1987), 308.

15. Conzen, "German Catholics in America," 580; Shaw, "The Cities and the Plains," 308.

16. M. Mark Stolarik, "Slovak Catholics in America," in *The Encyclopedia of American Catholic History*, 1324.

17. Finke and Stark, *The Churching of America*, 127.

18. Ibid., 117.

19. Mary Elizabeth Brown, "Italian Catholics in America," in *The Encyclopedia of American Catholic History*, 711.

20. Farnham and Bradley, "French Canadian Catholics in the United States," 549–53.

21. Conzen, "German Catholics in America," 576. The German figures are for 1869.

22. McCaffrey, "Irish Catholics in America," 699.

23. Diaz-Stevens, *Oxcart Catholicism on Fifth Avenue*, 72.

24. Ellen Skerrett, "The Irish in Chicago: The Catholic Dimension," in *Catholicism, Chicago Style,* ed. Ellen Skerrett, Edward R. Kantowicz, and Steven M. Avella (Chicago: Loyola University Press, 1993), 31.

25. Shaw, "The Cities and the Plains," 313.

26. Diaz-Stevens, *Oxcart Catholicism on Fifth Avenue*, 131.

27. Edward R. Kantowicz, "The Ethnic Church," in *Catholicism, Chicago Style*, 12.

28. Edward R. Kantowicz, "Cardinal Mundelein of Chicago and the Shaping of Twentieth-Century American Catholicism," in *Catholicism, Chicago Style*, 74.

29. Ellen Skerrett, "Sacred Space: Parish and Neighborhood in Chicago," in *Catholicism, Chicago Style,* 154.

30. Ellen Skerrett, "The Irish in Chicago," in *Catholicism, Chicago Style,* 53.

31. Hosffman Ospino, "Hispanic Ministry in Catholic Parishes" (Boston College School of Theology and Ministry, 2014), 7.

32. Mark Gray, "The Hispanic Population in Catholic Dioceses," *Nineteen Sixty-four* (blog), http://nineteenysixty-four.blogspot.com.

33. Diaz-Stevens, *Oxcart Catholicism on Fifth Avenue*, 12, 23.

34. Kantowicz, "The Ethnic Church," in *Catholicism, Chicago Style*, 25.

35. Ibid, 26.

36. Diaz-Stevens, *Oxcart Catholicism on Fifth Avenue*, 85.

37. Ibid., 6.

38. Nancy J. Wellmeier, "Santa Eulalia's People in Exile: Maya Religion, Culture and Identity in Los Angeles," in *Gatherings in Diaspora: Religious Communities and*

the New Immigration, ed. R. Stephen Warner and Judith G. Wittner (Philadelphia: Temple University Press, 1998), 105.

39. Ibid., 114.

40. Kantowicz, "The Ethnic Church," in *Catholicism, Chicago Style*, 26.

41. Diaz-Stevens, *Oxcart Catholicism on Fifth Avenue*, 108.

42. Wellmeier, "Santa Eulalia's People in Exile," 98.

43. Diaz-Stevens, *Oxcart Catholicism on Fifth Avenue*, 159, describes one such attempt—the transformation by the New York Archdiocese of the Puerto Rican *Fiesta de San Juan* into the *Fiesta de la Comunidad Hispana.* It ended up by attracting neither Puerto Ricans nor non-Puerto Ricans.

44. Mark Gray, Melissa Cidade, Mary Gautier, and Thomas Gaunt, SJ, "Cultural Diversity in the Catholic Church in the United States," Center for Applied Research in the Apostolate (Georgetown University, 2013).

45. James Stuart Olson, *Catholic Immigrants in America* (Chicago: Nelson-Hall, 1987), 164.

46. Simon C. Kim, *Memory and Honor: Cultural and Generational Ministry with Korean American Communities* (Collegeville, MN: Liturgical Press, 2010), 10.

47. R. Stephan Warner, "Introduction: Immigration and Religious Communities in the United States," in *Gatherings in Diaspora*, 6.

48. Ospino, "Hispanic Ministry in Catholic Parishes," 17.

Chapter 2: Catholicism through Ethnic Eyes—(pages 25–35)

1. Elizabeth McAlister, "The Madonna of 115th Street Revisited," in Warner and Wittner, *Gatherings in Diaspora*, 139.

2. Olson, *Catholic Immigrants in America*, 150.

3. Kim, *Memory and Honor*, 62. According to William Biernatzki in *Roots of Acceptance, han* is one of the root paradigms of Korean culture.

4. Ibid., 63.

5. Ibid., 101.

6. Robert Anthony Orsi, *The Madonna of 115th Street: Faith and Community in Italian Harlem, 1880-1950* (New Haven, CT: Yale University Press, 1985), chap. 4. Orsi notes that religious order priests, brothers, and sisters were *not* subject to this suspicion because they were attached to a community that served as their family.

7. See, for example, Caroline B. Brettell, "The Priest and His People: The Contractual Basis for Religious Practice in Rural Portugal," and Ruth Behar, "The Struggle for the Church: Popular Anticlericalism and Religiosity in Post-Franco Spain," both in *Religious Orthodoxy and Popular Faith in European Society*, ed. Ellen Badone (Princeton, NJ: Princeton University Press, 1990). See also Olson, *Catholic Immigrants in America*, 151, for Mexican Catholics. The Irish, Poles, and Germans, on the other hand, gave their priests more power and respect.

8. Wellmeier, "Saint Eulalia's People in Exile," 106.

9. Shaw, "The Cities and the Plains," 309.

10. Wellmeier, "Saint Eulalia's People in Exile," 111.

11. Sister Loyola, SBS, 1906. Annals of the Sisters of the Blessed Sacrament, in *The Frontiers and Catholic Identities,* ed. Anne M. Butler, Michael E. Engh, Thomas W. Spalding (Maryknoll, NY: Orbis, 1999), 204–5.

12. Diaz-Stevens, *Oxcart Catholicism on Fifth Avenue,* 114.

13. Kim, *Memory and Honor,* 85.

14. Diaz-Stevens, *Oxcart Catholicism on Fifth Avenue,* 114.

15. Silvano M. Tomasi, *Piety and Power: The Role of Italian Parishes in the New York Metropolitan Area* (New York: Center for Migration Studies, 1975), 124.

16. McAlister, "The Madonna of 115th Street Revisted," in Warner and Wittner, *Gatherings in Diaspora,* 126.

17. See Diaz-Stevens, *Oxcart Catholicism on Fifth Avenue,* 159–63, for the Puerto Rican celebration; Colleen McDannell, "True Men as We Need Them," *American Studies* 26 (Fall 1986): 19–36, for the Irish St. Patrick's Day parades; and Ramon A. Gutierrez, "El Santuario de Chimayo," in *Feasts and Celebrations in North American Ethnic Communities,* ed. Ramon A. Gutierrez and Genevieve Fabre (Albuquerque, NM: University of New Mexico Press, 1995), 71–86, for Chimayo.

18. Wellmeier, "Saint Eulalia's People in Exile," 106.

19. Ibid., 112.

20. It is no accident that major Catholic holy days—Christmas, Candlemas Day, the feasts of the Annunciation and Assumption, and Halloween/All Saints Day—occur on the solstices and the equinox, as well as on the "cross quarter days" between them, days that were sacred in pre-Christian European religions.

21. Japonica Brown-Saracino, "Social Preservationists and the Quest for Authentic Community," *City & Community* 3, no. 2 (2004): 153. See also McAlister, "The Madonna of 115th Street Revisited," 138, who makes this point about Haitians.

22. McDannell, "True Men as We Need Them," *American Studies* 26, 25.

23. See McAlister, "The Madonna of 115th Street Revisited," 144, home rituals among the Haitians; Diaz-Stevens, *Oxcart Catholicism on Fifth Avenue,* 6, for Puerto Ricans; Kim, *Memory and Honor,* 39, 97, for Koreans; and Olson, *Catholic Immigrants in America,* 159, for Filipinos.

24. Quoted in Philip Kasinitz, "New York Equalize You: The Political Economy of New York's West Indian Community," *New York Affairs* (January 1987).

25. L. Viki Ruiz, "'It's the People Who Drive the Book:' A View from the West," *American Quarterly* 46 (June 1993): 243-48, 246.

26. Pope Francis, *Evangelii Gaudium,* 122.

27. Diaz-Stevens, *Oxcart Catholicism on Fifth Avenue,* 151–52.

28. Pope Francis, *Evangelii Gaudium,* 122.

29. Ibid., 126.

Chapter 3: Welcoming Ethnic Cultures—(pages 36–54)

1. Robert D. Putnam and David E. Campbell, *American Grace: How Religion Divides and Unites Us* (New York: Simon and Schuster, 2010), 292.

2. Committee on Cultural Diversity in the Church, "Building Intercultural Competence for Ministers" (Washington, DC: United States Conference of Catholic Bishops, 2012), 1. In some areas, the percentage is much higher: one 2009 study found that 71 percent of parishes in the Archdiocese of Miami and 52 percent of parishes in the Diocese of Oakland offered Masses in more than one language. This study is cited in Bret C. Hoover, CSP, "The Shared Parish," *The American Catholic Studies Newsletter* (The Cushwa Center for the Study of American Catholicism) 37, no. 2 (Fall 2010): 7.

3. Hoover, "The Shared Parish," 1–2.

4. Ospino, "Hispanic Ministry in Catholic Parishes," 16.

5. We would, for example, object to an ethnic group that liked to eat kittens, or whose festival involved dancing naked in the streets.

6. Periodically, of course, Quebec threatens to secede and form a separate nation.

7. Committee on Cultural Diversity in the Church, "Best Practices for Shared Parishes" (Washington, DC: United States Conference of Catholic Bishops, 2013), 2–4.

8. Michael White and Tom Corcoran, *Rebuilt: Awakening the Faithful, Reaching the Lost, Making Church Matter* (Notre Dame, IN: Ave Maria, 2013), 43–44.

9. Committee on Cultural Diversity in the Church, "Best Practices for Shared Parishes," 2–4.

10. Ibid., 27.

11. Committee on Cultural Diversity in the Church, "Building Intercultural Competence for Ministers," 9.

12. Diaz-Stevens, *Oxcart Catholicism on Fifth Avenue*, 114.

13. Kim, *Memory and Honor*, 85.

14. Sheba George, "Caroling with the Keralites: The Negotiation of Gendered Space in an Indian Immigrant Church," in Warner and Wittner, *Gatherings in Diaspora*, 265–94.

15. Geert Hofstede, *Culture's Consequences: Comparing Values, Behaviors, Institutions, and Organizations across Nations* (Thousand Oaks, CA: Sage, 2001), cited in "Building Intercultural Competence for Ministers," 10–12.

16. We don't, in fact, even have a vocabulary to talk about the needs or operations of a group apart from the individuals that compose it—not in economics, nor in political science, nor in religion. See Patricia Wittberg, *Building Strong Church Communities: A Sociological Overview* (Mahwah, NJ: Paulist, 2012).

17. The Barna Group, "The Longer Hispanics Experience U.S. Culture, the Less Socially Conservative They Become" (August 20, 2013), http://hispanics.barna .org/.

18. "Hispanic Catholics and Protestants Compared on Social Attitudes," *The CARA Report* 7, no. 4 (Spring 2002): 9, and "Current Research," *Religion Watch* 29, no. 8 (June 2014): 6.

19. Frank Newport, "U.S. Catholic Hispanic Population Less Religious, Shrinking" (February 25, 2013), http://www.gallup.com/poll/160691/.

20. Ibid.

21. Ibid.

22. Ospino, "Hispanic Ministry in Catholic Parishes," 41.

23. Ibid., 36.

24. Diaz-Stevens, *Oxcart Catholicism on Fifth Avenue*, 205.

25. Allan Figueroa Deck, SJ, "The Challenge of Evangelical/Pentecostal Christianity to Hispanic Catholicism in the United States," Cushwa Center Working Paper Series 24, no. 1 (Notre Dame, IN: University of Notre Dame, 1992): 25.

26. Edmundo Rodriguez, SJ, "Realities for Hispanics," *Company* (Fall 1988): 9.

27. Ibid., 10.

28. Luis Leon, "Born Again in East LA: The Congregation as Border Space," in Warner and Wittner, *Gatherings in Diaspora*, 188.

29. Deck, "Challenge of Evangelical/Pentecostal Christianity," 22–23.

30. Leon, "Born Again in East LA," 191.

31. Ibid., 178.

32. Ibid., 188.

33. Ibid., 188.

34. Gerardo Marin and Raymond J. Gamba, "The Role of Expectations in Religious Conversions: The Case of Hispanic Catholics," *Review of Religious Research* 34, no. 4 (June 1993): 369.

35. And not just Hispanic ethnic groups, either: Kim, *Memory and Honor*, 85, notes a similar practice among Korean Catholics.

36. Diaz-Stevens, *Oxcart Catholicism on Fifth Avenue*, 128, makes this point about Puerto Rican Catholics in New York.

37. Wittberg, *Building Strong Church Communities*, 150.

38. Committee on Cultural Diversity in the Church, "Best Practices for Shared Parishes," 44.

39. Hoover, "The Shared Parish," 8.

40. Diaz-Stevens, *Oxcart Catholicism on Fifth Avenue*, 56.

41. "Member Services in Chicago Latino Congregations," *The CARA Report*, 19, no. 3 (Winter 2014): 7.

42. The question wording was "Has this church or someone from this church ever helped you or your family in the following ways: Provided food or clothing. Helped find a job. Helped with a financial need. Helped find a house or apartment."

43. Committee on Cultural Diversity in the Church, "Best Practices for Shared Parishes," 35.

44. Ospino, "Hispanic Ministry in Catholic Parishes," 42.

45. Ibid., 25–26.

46. Diaz-Stephens, *Oxcart Catholicism on Fifth Avenue*, 197.

47. Kim, *Memory and Honor,* 19, 73.

48. Committee on Cultural Diversity in the Church, "Best Practices for Shared Parishes," 25.

49. Bill Kenkelen, "Culture seen as key to keeping Hispanics in church," *National Catholic Reporter* (April 13, 1990): 7.

50. Hoover, "The Shared Parish," 9.

51. M. P. Baumgartner, *The Moral Order of a Suburb* (New York: Oxford University Press, 1988), 3.

52. Committee on Cultural Diversity in the Church, "Building Intercultural Competence for Ministers," 19.

53. Committee on Cultural Diversity in the Church, "Best Practices for Shared Parishes," 19.

54. Ibid., 19.

55. Cited in Diaz-Stevens, *Oxcart Catholicism on Fifth Avenue*, 169.

Chapter 4: Generational Cultures: An Overview—(pages 55–68)

1. Anthony Esler, "'The Truest Community': Social Generations as Collective Mentalities," *Journal of Political and Military Sociology* 12 (Spring 1984): 99–112, 106. See also June Edmunds and Bryan S. Turner, "Global Generations: Social Change in the Twentieth Century," *The British Journal of Sociology* 56, no. 4:559-577 (2005): 566, who use the term "collective memory" to describe a similar concept.

2. Marvin Rintala, "Political Generations," in the *International Encyclopedia of the Social Sciences*, vol. 6:92-96 (New York: Macmillan and the Free Press, 1968), 93.

3. Jean M. Twenge, *Generation Me: Why Today's Young Americans Are More Confident, Assertive, Entitled—and More Miserable Then Ever Before* (New York: Free Press, 2006), 8.

4. Chris Mooney, "The Science of Why We Don't Believe Science," Mother Jones (April 18, 2011), http://motherjones.com/print/106166.

5. See Philip Converse, "The Nature of Belief Systems in Mass Publics," in *Ideology and Discontent,* ed. David E. Apter (New York: Free Press, 1964), 206–45, for the seminal discussion of "packages" of unrelated ideological beliefs.

6. Howard Schuman and Jacqueline Scott, "Generations and Collective Memories," *American Sociological Review* 54, no. 3 (1989): 359–81.

7. D. Michael Lindsey, *Faith in the Halls of Power: How Evangelicals Joined the American Elite* (New York: Oxford University Press, 2007).

8. Edmunds and Turner, "Global Generations: Social Change in the Twentieth Century," 562.

9. Jane Pilcher, "Mannheim's Sociology of Generations: An Undervalued Legacy," *The British Journal of Sociology* 45, no. 3 (1994): 487.

10. Robert S. Laufer and Vern L. Bengtson, "Generations, Aging, and Social Stratification: On the Development of Generational Units," *Journal of Social Issues* 30, no. 3 (1974): 181–205.

11. David D. Burstein, *Fast Future: How the Millennial Generation Is Shaping Our World* (Boston: Beacon, 2013), 140.

12. Robin Marantz Henig and Samantha Henig, *Twenty Something: Why Do Young Adults Seem Stuck?* (New York: Penguin, 2012), xvii.

13. Mike Hayes, *Googling God: The Religious Landscape of People in Their 20s and 30s* (Mahwah, NJ: Paulist, 2007), 6.

14. Jean M. Twenge, *Generation Me* (New York: Free Press, 2006). See also John Tierney, "A Generation's Vanity, Heard Through Lyrics," *New York Times,* April 25, 2011.

15. Arthur Levine and Diane R. Dean, "Ways Today's Students Are Radically Changing Our Colleges," *Trusteeship,* November/December 2013, 27–30.

16. Henig and Henig, *Twenty Something*, 206.

17. John H. Pryor et al., "The American Freshman: Forty Year Trends," Cooperative Institutional Research Program, Higher Education Research Institute, UCLA, 52–53. Accessed via http://gseis.ucla.edu/heri/PDFs/40TrendsManuscript.pdf.

18. Which is not the same as saying they eschew premarital sex: on the contrary, two-thirds of Millennial brides are already living with the groom on their wedding day. See Henig and Henig, *Twenty Something*, 95.

19. Marc Prensky, "Digital Natives, Digital Immigrants," *On the Horizon* 9:5 (2001): 1–6.

20. Michael Wolff, "Massive Media," *USA Weekend* (July 11–13, 2014): 6–7.

21. Christian Smith, *Lost in Transition: The Dark Side of Emerging Adulthood* (New York: Oxford, 2011), 27–47.

22. Pew Research Center, "Young, Underemployed and Optimistic" (February 9, 2012), www.pewsocialtrends.org.

23. Riva Froymovich, *End of the Good Life: How the Financial Crisis Threatens a Lost Generation, and What We Can Do about It* (New York: Harper, 2013), 29.

24. Pew Research Center, "Millennials in Adulthood: Detached from Institutions, Networked with Friends" (March 7, 2014), 9.

25. Henig and Henig, *Twenty Something*, 31–32.

26. Pew Research Center, "Young, Underemployed and Optimistic," 29; Pew Research Center, "Millennials in Adulthood," 8. See also Froymovich, *End of the Good Life,* 39, and Burstein, *Fast Future,* 49. Only 46 percent of their Baby Boomer parents share the Millennials' optimism about their future.

27. Smith, *Lost in Transition*, 150.

28. Froymovich, *End of the Good Life*, 190.

29. Burstein, *Fast Future,* 112.

30. Ibid., 37, 178.

31. Ibid., 96.

32. Sherry Turkle, *Alone Together: Why We Expect More from Technology and Less from Each Other* (New York: Basic, 2011), 189–91.

33. David Brooks, "The Empirical Kids," *New York Times* (March 28, 2013), http://www.nytimes.com/2013/03/29/opinion/brooks-the-empirical-kids.html.

34. Turkle, *Alone Together,* 190–91.

35. Quoted in Burstein, *Fast Future,* 68.

36. Turkle, *Alone Together,* 248.

37. Some writers also speak of a "One-and-a-Half Generation": persons born abroad but brought here as infants or as very small, preschool, children.

38. Often, they have only a "passive" understanding of the language: they understand it when spoken but cannot speak it themselves. And they certainly can't read or write it.

39. This obviously does not apply to ethnic groups, such as African Americans, who have been actively discriminated against and forced by white racism to develop a "dual consciousness" of being primarily BLACK Americans. Third-generation immigrants from the African Diaspora, such as immigrants from the West Indies or from Africa itself, often assimilate to African American culture.

40. Liston Pope, *Millhands and Preachers: A Study of Gastonia* (New Haven, CT: Yale University Press, 1942).

41. C. Eric Lincoln and Lawrence H. Mamiya, *The Black Church in the African American Experience* (Durham, NC: Duke University Press, 1990).

Chapter 5: Generational Cultures in the US Catholic Church— (pages 69–82)

1. See, for example, William V. D'Antonio, James D. Davidson, Dean R. Hoge, and Mary L. Gautier, *American Catholics Today: New Realities of Their Faith and Their Church* (Lanham, MD: Rowman & Littlefield, 2007), 98–101.

2. William V. D'Antonio, Michele Dillon, and Mary L. Gautier, *American Catholics in Transition* (Lanham, MD: Rowman and Littlefield, 2013), 21, 58. "Highly committed" Catholics answered "The most important part of my life" when asked how important the Catholic Church was to them personally, went to Mass at least weekly, and rated themselves as highly unlikely ever to leave the church.

3. Ibid., 22.

4. Christian Smith and Patricia Snell, *Souls in Transition: The Religious and Spiritual Lives of Emerging Adults* (New York: Oxford, 2009), 91. See also Vern L. Bengtson, *Families and Faith: How Religion Is Passed Down Across Generations* (New

York: Oxford University Press, 2013), 58. Bengtson calls the Catholic intergenerational decline "eye-popping."

5. D'Antonio, Dillon, and Gautier, *American Catholics in Transition,* 21.

6. Ibid., 26.

7. See A. O. Hirschman, *Exit, Voice, and Loyalty: Responses to Decline in Firms, Organizations, and States* (Cambridge, MA: Harvard University Press, 1970), for a theoretical discussion of the motivations behind exiting or staying in an organization.

8. Melissa A. Cidade, "Young Adult Catholics and the Church," (presentation at the Romero Center in Camden, NJ, May 29, 2011), Center for Applied Research in the Apostolate. See also Mark Gray, "C and E Catholics Decoded," *Nineteen Sixty-four* (blog), Center for Applied Research in the Apostolate, September 6, 2011, http://www.nineteensixty-four.blogspot.com/search?updated-min=2011-01-01T00:00:00-05:00&updated-max=2012-01-01T00:00:00-05:00&max-results=33. Between 58 percent and 64 percent of Vatican II, post-Vatican II, and Millennial Catholics attend Mass only a few times a year; only 36 percent of pre-Vatican II Catholics attend that rarely.

9. James D. Davidson, Andrea S. Williams, Richard A. Lamanna, Jan Stenftenagel, Kathleen Maas Weigert, William J. Whalen, and Patricia Wittberg, *The Search for Common Ground: What Unites and Divides Catholic Americans* (Huntington, IN: Our Sunday Visitor Press, 1997), 126, 130.

10. Bengtson, *Families and Faith*, 31, and John P. Hoffman, "Declining Religious Authority? Confidence in the Leaders of Religious Organizations, 1973-2010," *Review of Religious Research* 55, no. 1 (2013): 1–25.

11. Bengston, *Families and Faith,* 36.

12. Christian Smith, Kyle Longest, Jonathan Hill, and Kari Christoffersen, *Young Catholic America: Emerging Adults In, Out of, and Gone from the Church (*New York: Oxford University Press, 2014), 26.

13. Ibid., 23.

14. Tom Beaudoin, *Virtual Faith: The Irreverent Spiritual Quest of Generation X* (San Francisco: Jossey-Bass, 1998), 41.

15. Davidson et al., *Search for Common Ground*, 127.

16. Mark Silk, "Gen-X Catholic Debacle," Religion News Service (June 5, 2012), http://www.religionnews.com/blogs/mark-silk/gen-x-catholic-debacle.

17. Christian Smith, with Melinda Lundquist Denton, *Soul Searching: The Religious and Spiritual Lives of American Teenagers* (New York: Oxford University Press, 2005), 289.

18. Ibid.

19. Putnam and Campbell, *American Grace* (New York: Simon and Schuster, 2010), 41–42; David E. Campbell and Robert D. Putnam, "God and Caesar in America," *Foreign Affairs* 91, no. 2 (2012): 34-43.

20. Gabe Lyons, *The Next Christians* (New York: Random House, 2010), 40, and Sarah Wilkins LaFlamme, "Toward Religious Polarization? Time Effects on Reli-

gious Commitment in the U.S., U.K., and Canadian Regions," *Sociology of Religion* 75, no. 2 (2014): 287. According to Harvard University's Institute of Politics, in their Survey of Young Americans' Attitudes toward Politics and Public Service," barely 20 percent of Millennials agreed that religious values should play a more important role in government, while close to 50 percent disagreed—one-third strongly.

21. David Kinnaman and Gabe Lyons, *UnChristian: What a New Generation Really Thinks about Christianity* (Grand Rapids, MI: Baton, 2007), 24, 26, 28, 125.

22. Robert P. Jones, Daniel Cox, and Thomas Banchoff, *A Generation in Transition: Religion, Values, and Politics among College-Age Millennials* (Washington, DC: Public Religion Research Institute, 2012), 7.

23. Bengtson, *Families and Faith,* 58.

24. Mark Gray, "Young Adult Catholics Haven't Lost God's Number," *Nineteen Sixty-four* (blog), Center for Applied Research in the Apostolate, http://www .nineteensixty-four.blogspot.com/. See also Pew Forum on Religion and Public Life, "Faith in Flux: Changes in Religious Affiliation in the U.S." (Washington, DC: Pew Research Center, 2009), 21, and Smith and Snell, *Souls in Transition,* 109.

25. Cidade, "Young Adult Catholics and the Church." See also Philip Schwadel, "Changes in Americans' Strength of Religious Affiliation, 1974-2010," *Sociology of Religion,* 74, no. 1 (2013): 125.

26. Smith and Denton, *Soul Searching,* 37–40.

27. Ibid., 46, 51, 53, 60, 64.

28. D'Antonio et al., *American Catholics Today,* 98-101.

29. Smith and Denton, *Soul Searching,* 40, 209.

30. Ibid., 66; Smith and Snell, *Souls in Transition,* 140.

31. Smith and Denton, *Soul Searching,* 141.

32. Ibid., 162–70.

33. Among them are "Abiders/Adapters/Assenters/Avoiders/Atheists" (Lisa Pearce and Melinda Lundquist Denton, *A Faith of Their Own* [New York: Oxford, 2011], 55); "Devoted/Regulars/Sporadic/Disengaged" (Smith and Denton, *Soul Searching,* 219–20); "Eclipsed/Private/Ecumenical/Evangelical/Sacramental" (Hayes, *Googling God,* 14); "Church in Mission/in Search/Youthful/Apologist/Devotional/ Busy/Creative/Disconnected" (Mary Ann Reese, "Refracting the Light," *America* [September 22, 2003]); and "Committed Traditionalists/Selective Adherents/Spiritually Open/Religiously Indifferent/Religiously Disconnected/Irreligious" (Smith and Snell, *Souls in Transition,* 167–69).

34. Smith and Snell, *Souls in Transition,* 304.

35. Ibid., 167, 304. See also Dean R. Hoge et al., *Young Adult Catholics: Religion in the Culture of Choice* (Notre Dame, IN: Notre Dame University Press, 2001), 71.

36. D'Antonio et al., *American Catholics in Transition,* 58. See also Schwadel, "Changes in Americans' Strength of Religious Affiliation, 1974-2010," 107–8.

37. D. Paul Sullins, "Institutional Selection for Conformity: The Case of U.S. Catholic Priests," *Sociology of Religion,* 74, no.1 (2013): 56-81; Mary L. Gautier, Paul

M. Perl, and Stephen J. Fichter, *Same Call, Different Men: The Evolution of the Priesthood Since Vatican II* (Collegeville, MN: Liturgical Press, 2012), 87; Dean R. Hoge and Jacqueline E. Wenger, *Evolving Visions of the Priesthood: Changes from Vatican II to the Turn of the New Century* (Collegeville, MN: Liturgical Press, 2003), 132–33.

38. Hayes, *Googling God*, 153–54; Hoffman, "Declining Religious Authority," 21.

39. Hayes, *Googling God*, 154.

40. Lyons, *The Next Christians*, 38.

41. Hoge and Wenger, *Evolving Visions of the Priesthood*, 118; Dean R. Hoge and Marti R. Jewell, *The Next Generation of Pastoral Leaders: What the Church Needs to Know* (Chicago: Loyola University Press, 2010), 85.

42. Sullins, "Institutional Selection for Conformity," 56–81.

43. Hoffman, "Declining Religious Authority," 20.

44. LaFlamme, "Toward Religious Polarization?" 302.

45. See Figure 1, page 5.

46. D'Antonio et al., *American Catholics in Transition*, 143.

47. Ibid., 144.

48. "Foreign-Born Hispanics Are More Socially Conservative" *The CARA Report*, Center for Applied Research in the Apostolate, 19, no. 3 (Winter 2014): 8.

49. D'Antonio et al., *American Catholics in Transition*, 145.

50. Ospino, "Hispanic Ministry in Catholic Parishes," 8.

51. Pyong Gap Min and Dae Young Kim, "Intergenerational Transmission of Religion and Culture: Korean Protestants in the U.S.," *Sociology of Religion*, 66, no. 3 (2005): 267.

52. Ibid., 268.

53. Kim, *Memory and Honor*, 52.

54. Ibid., 81.

55. Ibid., 47.

56. Patricia Wittberg, "Religious Practice at the Intersection of Generation and Gender: A Case Study of American Catholicism," paper read at the annual meeting of the Religious Research Association, Boston, November 9, 2013.

57. Davidson et al., *Search for Common Ground*, 141–54. See also Wittberg, *Building Strong Church Communities*, 125, 180.

58. D'Antonio et al., *American Catholics in Transition*, 91–92. See also Schwadel, "Changes in Americans' Strength of Religious Affiliation, 1974–2010," 122.

59. D'Antonio et al., *American Catholics in Transition*, 95–96, 149.

60. Ibid., 148.

61. Wittberg, "Religious Practice at the Intersection of Generation and Gender," paper read at the Annual Meeting of the Religious Research Association, Boston, MA, November 9, 2013.

62. D'Antonio et al., *American Catholics in Transition*, 96.

63. Ibid., 94.

64. "A New Catholic Subculture?" *The CARA Report* 19, no. 3 (Winter 2014): 11. See also Mark M. Gray, "Exclusive Analysis: National Catholic Marriage Rate Plummets," *Our Sunday Visitor* (June 26, 2011), http://www.osv.com/.

65. D'Antonio et al., *American Catholics in Transition*, 108.

66. "Declining Proportion of Baptisms a Cause for Concern," *The CARA Report* 19, no.1 (Summer 2013): 3.

67. Smith, Longest et al, *Young Catholic America*, 71.

68. Mark M. Gray and Mary L. Gautier, "Consideration of Priesthood and Religious Life among Never-Married U.S. Catholics" (Washington, DC: Center for Applied Research in the Apostolate, 2012), 9, 78, 99. See also Mary E. Bendyna and Mary L. Gautier, "Recent Vocations to Religious Life: A Report for the National Religious Vocation Conference" (Washington, DC: Center for Applied Research in the Apostolate, 2009), 25–27.

69. Hoge and Jewell, *Next Generation of Pastoral Leaders*, 13, 18.

70. Michael White and Tom Corcoran, *Rebuilt: Awakening the Faithful, Reaching the Lost, Making Church Matter* (Notre Dame, IN: Ave Maria, 2013), 225.

71. Members of the Ephrata Community, for example, nursed George Washington's army at Valley Forge.

72. Kai Erickson, *Everything in Its Path: The Destruction of Community in the Buffalo Creek Flood* (New York: Simon and Schuster, 1976).

73. Wittberg, "Religious Practice at the Intersection of Generation and Gender," 11–13. Millennial Catholic men, however, scored lower than older Catholic men on these measures.

74. Davidson et al., *Search for Common Ground*, 99–107.

Chapter 6: Welcoming Generational Cultures—(pages 83–98)

1. Reported in *Religion Watch* (April 2014), 5. This is a summary of the website for British Religion in Numbers (BRIN), http://www.brin.ac.uk/.

2. "In U.S., Rise in Religious 'Nones' Slows in 2012," http://www.gallup.com/poll/159785/rise-religious-nones-slows-2012.aspx%231.

3. D'Antonio et al., *American Catholics in Transition*, 117.

4. "A New Catholic Subculture?" *The CARA Report*, Center for Applied Research in the Apostolate 19, no. 3 (Winter 2014): 11.

5. Hoge and Jewell, *The Next Generation of Pastoral Leaders*, 120. The top recommendation of all respondents was the same: that the church pay more attention to young people. Note that this study was *not* a random sample. The authors surveyed only Catholic Millennials who were in some way known to parish youth ministers and college campus ministers. Thus, they were likely to have missed those Millennial Catholics who were less involved in the church.

6. Janet Fang, "People Would Rather Experience An Electric Shock Than Be Alone With Their Thoughts," http://www.iflscience.com/brain/people-would-rather-experience-electric-shock-be-alone-their-thoughts.

7. Neil Howe and William Strauss, *Millennials Rising: The Next Great Generation* (New York: Random House, 2000), 170–71.

8. Beaudoin, *Virtual Faith*, 38.

9. According to Christian Smith and Patricia Snell in *Souls in Transition*, 209, 226, 233, 286, Millennials attach an especially high significance to personal relationships in their religious practice.

10. Wittberg, *Building Strong Church Communities*, 127.

11. Smith and Snell, *Souls in Transition*, 45, 49, 51.

12. Kinnaman and Lyons, *UnChristian*, 182.

13. Edward P. Hahnenberg, "Commentary," in *The Next Generation of Pastoral Leaders*, Hoge and Jewell, 153–54.

14. Christian Smith, in *American Evangelicalism: Embattled and Thriving* (Chicago: University of Chicago Press, 1998), makes this argument about Protestant Evangelicals. Russell Shaw, in *American Church: The Remarkable Rise, Meteoric Fall, and Uncertain Future of Catholicism in America* (San Francisco: Ignatius, 2013), makes the argument about Catholic conservatives.

15. Putnam and Campbell, in *American Grace* 142, note that the percentage of Millennials who join Evangelical churches has fallen drastically.

16. Michael Hornsby-Smith, *The Changing Parish: A Study of Parishes, Priests, and Parishioners after Vatican II* (New York: Routledge, 1989), 66.

17. Kinnaman and Lyons, *UnChristian*, 130.

18. And which many in this minority see as the sole hope for the future of American Catholicism—which "writes off" the majority of Millennials and Post-Millennials. See Shaw, "The Cities and the Plains."

19. Hahnenberg, "Commentary," in *The Next Generation of Pastoral Leaders*, 154.

20. Henig and Henig, *Twentysomething*, 9.

21. Ibid., xiv. See also Smith and Snell, *Souls in Transition*, 53, who quote a young adult: "I've noticed a lot of people really upset and stressed not knowing what they want to do with their life. I know so many people that just get, like, broken down because they have no idea what they wanna do, where they wanna go."

22. Smith and Snell, *Souls in Transition*, 293.

23. Tara Parker-Pope, "Marital Bliss, One Decision after Another," *New York Times* (August 26, 2014): D1.

24. Kinnaman and Lyons, *UnChristian*, 103.

25. Hayes, *Googling God*, 141.

26. Ibid.

27. Turkle, *Alone Together*, 245.

28. Ibid., 201.

29. Ibid., 293. See page 345, footnote 29, for the author's citation of the research.

30. Ibid., 241.

31. Henig and Henig, *Twenty Something*, 180–81.

32. Ibid., 182.

33. Paul Jarzembowski, "Invite Overwhelmed Young Adults to Come, Rest in Christ," *Horizon* 38, no. 2 (Spring 2013): 15.

34. Patrick J. Brennan, *The Mission-Driven Parish* (New York: Orbis, 2007), 120.

35. Turkle, *Alone Together*, 266.

36. Hayes, *Googling God*, 27ff.

37. Ibid., 89.

38. Ibid., 144.

39. Smith et al., *Young Catholic America*, 169–70.

40. Smith and Snell, *Souls in Transition*, 285–86.

41. Kinnaman and Lyons, *UnChristian*, 134.

42. Hahnenberg, "Commentary," in *The Next Generation of Pastoral Leaders*, 155.

43. Hayes, *Googling God*, 36–37.

44. Brennan, *The Mission-Driven Parish*, 115–17.

45. Fran Caudron and Richard Rymarz, "Further Down the Road: Longitudinal Study or Retreat Leaders from Catholic Schools," *Review of Religious Research* 55 (2013): 529.

46. Hayes, *Googling God*, 134.

47. I suggest tactics and strategies for doing this in a previous book: Wittberg, *Building Strong Church Communities*, chap. 9.

48. Jarzembowski, "Invite Overwhelmed Young Adults to Come, Rest in Christ," 15.

49. Hayes, *Googling God*, 15.

50. Sherry Turkle, "The Documented Life," *New York Times*, December 15, 2013, http://www.nytimes.com.2013/12/16/opinion/the-documented-life.html.

51. Ibid.

52. Jarzembowski, "Invite Overwhelmed Young Adults to Come, Rest in Christ," 16.

53. Ibid., 16.

54. Turkle, *Alone Together*, 266–67.

55. Brennan, *The Mission-Driven Parish*, 45.

Conclusion—(pages 99–102)

1. Hahnenberg, "Commentary," in *The Next Generation of Pastoral Leaders,* Hoge and Jewell, 154.

2. Bengtson, *Families and Faith*, 190.

3. Ibid., 190.